Cover & Graphic Design

Mattias Långström

Contact: oneofakindbooks@bhagwan.se

Based on the Book

ASTRAL PROJECTION A COMPLETE GUIDE

by Secret WARLOCK

✹✹✹

Copyright © Mattias Långström

Publisher: ***BHAGWAN 2021***

No part of this publication may be reproduced or transmitted in any form, or by any means, electronic or mechanical, including photocopying, scanning, recording, or any information storage and retrieval system, without express written permission from the publisher, except for the inclusion of brief quotations embodied in critical articles and reviews. This book is a work of fiction and a product of the author´s imagination.

Index

Introduction

Astral projection, or as the English call it OBE (Out-of-Body-Experience), has millions of followers around the world. These followers believe that the soul is really separate from the body and that it is possible to detach oneself to a 4th dimension. The 4th dimension is a fantastic world where you can fly around and explore the earth or create whatever you want to create from the imagination. Many have experienced that they have woken up above their body, seen it lying there completely relaxed while involuntarily hovering above and wondered what is really going on, while others can consciously disconnect the soul from the body. A silver / blue string is then tied from the soul to the body, much like an umbilical cord. It makes the soul find its way back to the body after a flight through the world and it cannot be cut off, only if one dies. When you die, you automatically enter the 4th dimension and if you are good, you create a pleasant world for yourself, if you are evil, you create a world full of evil and fear.

Astral projection or astral projection (also including out-of-body experience means that the astral body (or a person's soul or consciousness) is separated from the physical body. This is said to occur or be achieved in a hypnagogic state or through dreams, deep meditation or drugs. The astral body can then travel to distant places or a parallel world called the astral plane, a supposedly higher level of consciousness. Astral projection is linked to both religious ideas about life after death, near-death experiences and the New Age movement.

To enable Astral travel, the chakras must be balanced and active. Ajna chakra, which is physically connected to the pineal gland, must be activated and cleansed so that you can become aware of the impressions and experiences you get to experience during the journey.

Good Luck and have a safe journey!

Psychic Mattias Långström

Chapter 1

WHAT IS THE ASTRAL REALM

Introduction

There are certain aspects of the astral dimension and the projection process that are very complicated- Much of it is misunderstood and it can all be very confusing at times. This series of articles attempts to shed a little light on the subject, and hopefully, explain what it's all about. The theories and conclusions in this Treatise are largely drawn from my own projection experience. It is the goal of this Treatise to develop greater understanding and new, simpler and more effective techniques for projection. The ideas, theories and techniques discussed here are constantly under development and are subject to modification and change as new discoveries and insights come to light.

What is the Astral Dimension?

The astral is the closest dimension to the physical. It overlays and permeates the world like a huge mind net, catching and holding all thought. Its contents are created by the collective consciousness of the world mind. It contains all the thoughts, memories, fantasies, and dreams of every living thing in the world. In it, the laws of sympathetic attraction, or like attracts like, causes this ocean of mind stuff to strata and settle into layers or pools. These pools of thought are more commonly called astral planes, astral worlds, astral sub planes or astral realms. The astral dimension is composed of astral matter and is aptly described as mind stuff. It is extremely sensitive to thought and can be moulded into any shape or form. These creations can be so perfect as to be indistinguishable from reality.

The best way to explain this, mind stuff is to draw a comparison between astral matter and unexposed, high speed photographic film. When this film is exposed to light, focused by the cameras lens, a perfect image of reality is instantly burnt into the film by the chemical reaction of the film to light.

When astral matter is exposed to thought, focused by the lens of the mind, a perfect image of reality is instantly formed out of astral mind stuff by the reaction of astral matter to thought. The complexity and durability of any creation in the astral dimension depends largely on the strength of the mind doing the creating.

Dreams

This is how the subconscious mind creates dreams: By tuning into the astral dimension during sleep, it can create any scenario it wishes. This is the subconscious mind's way of solving problems and of communicating with the conscious mind. It creates a series of complex thought form scenarios and projects them into the mind stuff of the astral dimension, where they become solid. The conscious mind then lives through and experiences these created scenarios in the dream state. In a way it's like a movie projector (subconscious mind) projecting onto a movie screen (astral dimension).

Thought Forms

Any new object in the real world is assimilated into the astral dimension over a period of time. A thought form representation of it first grows in the lowest part of the astral, close to the physical dimension, becoming more and more permanent as time goes on. As with all thought forms, the more attention paid to it the quicker it grows.

The higher up in the astral dimension, or the further away from the physical, the less thought forms, of the physical world, as we know it, are found.

Physical things have to soak in to it for a very long time before they take shape, and are found, in the higher astral.

Have you ever tried to move around a strange house in the dark? You bump into everything, right. But as you become familiar with it though, a mental picture of your surroundings forms in your mind, and you can find your way around it better. The longer you spend in this house the stronger this mental picture becomes. This is similar to how things are assimilated and grown, as thought forms, in other dimensions.

The generation of thought forms in the astral also works in the reverse. If a physical object has been around for a very long time, it will have grown a lasting thought form impression in the astral. After the object is destroyed or removed, its thought form still endures. You may, for example, in the astral, find furniture in your house you don't have, jumbled up with your own. This is caused by the decaying thought forms of old stuff, belonging to previous tenants etc., still being there, years after the originals have gone.

Old thought forms do not follow their physical counterpart around when they are moved. New ones begin to grow in the astral wherever it is while the old ones slowly decay. The longer a thing is in one place, the stronger the thought form will become in that place. This also applies to buildings, structures and geological features. You may project into a park and find a house, bridge, stream, hill etc. that you know is definitely not there. These may have existed in times past. The higher up in the astral you go, the older the thought forms are, or the further back in geological time you appear to be.

The rate of growth of a thought form depends largely on the amount of attention paid to it. For example, a famous painting; loved, viewed and highly thought of by millions, will have a much stronger thought form than that of a common painting that hangs in someone's bedroom and is only viewed by a few. The number of thought forms you find in the astral also depends on

*how close you are to the physical dimension. If you are
very close, as in a real time projection or OOBE, very
few thought forms, if any, will be found. In a real time
OOBE you are not quite in the astral dimension but are
existing as an astral form in the buffer zone between the
astral and the physical dimensions.*

Astral Vision

*in the physical body we have 220 degrees of vision, i.e.
we can only see in front of us, but not behind, above
and below at the same time. In the Astral body we have
MORE than 360 degrees of vision and can see on all
sides at once. This is Spherical vision. During projection,
habit forces us to focus our attention in one direction
only, where we feel the forward part of our vision
is. The view behind, above, below, left and right is still
there, and seen all at once, but it cannot be assimilated
by the brain, all at once. This goes against the brains
lifelong habit of frontal vision. Spherical vision is like
being one huge multi faceted eye that can see in all
directions, up, down, left, right, front, back, but all at
once! In the astral body you do not have any physical
organs, i.e., eyes. You are a non-physical point of consciousness floating in space. You are also unaffected by*

gravity and other laws of physics. In this state there are no ups or downs, backs or fronts, left or rights. It is only lifelong habit that tries to force this perspective on you during projection.

It is important to understand spherical vision, if you are to operate competently in the astral. This is especially so when you project, in real time, close to the physical dimension. Spherical vision will often cause you to think you are in a mirror image dimension, or a reversed copy of reality. This means your house, for example, will appear to be reversed, back to front.

This is caused by you losing your original natural viewpoint during projection. At some point during the projection you have become disoriented and taken a different viewpoint from normal, i.e., you have rotated or turned upside down or inside without thinking. This reverses your natural left right, up down viewpoint. This tricks the subconscious mind into reversing the place you are in so your conscious mind can function properly. As you don't have a physical body in the astral, if you want to look behind yourself you don't have to turn around, or move at all. You just change your viewpoint to the rear. This, when done without moving, causes the mirror image effect, in a way it's like looking in a mirror to see behind.

This causes the subconscious mind to use its creative power to correct the view by reversing it, or parts of it. This is easier and causes fewer problems for the conscious mind than if it had to try and accept a reversal of left and right.

A similar effect can be had by lying down and looking above your head, or standing on your head and trying to pick the left and right sides of things.

This causes a slight confusion in your sense of left and right, i.e., you have to consciously calculate which is left and right from your reversed position. This slight confusion is all that is needed to trick the subconscious mind into creating something easier to accept.

Your brain is unable to assimilate this reversal and thus gives you a new perspective according to what it feels is left and right at the time. Once you consciously notice this anomaly it is too late to reverse it. The brain cannot accept a conscious change of left and right.

If you understand spherical vision though, and happen to get reversed sometime during a projection, it is no longer a problem. You can take it into account and function normally, rather than thinking you are wasting your time in some strange mirror dimension, i.e., if you had plans to do something in the astral you still can. All you have to do is, take your left right coordinates from the building or structure around you, and ignore your own sense of left and right completely.

Everything you see while you are in the astral dimension is directly perceived by the mind. It is a simple matter for the subconscious mind to twist or reverse, all, or even part of, your conscious perception of reality during a projection.

Note: This reversal of viewpoint can happen many times during any one real time projection.

Creative Visualisation Power

The subconscious mind has VASTLY greater powers of visualisation than the conscious mind. It is like comparing a super computer to a child's calculator.

In the astral dimension, during any conscious projection or lucid dream, where the conscious mind is aware, this difference can cause great confusion. The subconscious mind simmers beneath the surface during any projection. All that creative power is just bursting to get out, to create and it will do just that any chance it gets. This difference in creative power, combined with the lifelong habit of normal frontal vision, is the cause of the "Alice in Wonderland Effect." Let me explain....

Take these together:

1. The incredible creative power of the subconscious mind.
2. The weak creative powers of the conscious mind.
3. The sensitivity of astral matter to thought.
4. Spherical vision.
5. Left, right sense reversals.

And you have a recipe for total confusion.

The Alice in Wonderland Effect
You project your astral body and look around your room. Everything appears normal, but suddenly, you notice the door is on the wrong wall?

While looking around, you have seen this door with your rear vision, confusing your natural left, right, brain perspective. The brain can't assimilate this because your frontal perspective, and the position of the furniture, pictures, windows etc., are normal; but the view behind you is reversed. This tricks the subconscious mind into creating a door where it thinks it should be. When you look at this door, it appears real, even though you know it is in the wrong place. Once it has been created, it will not be uncreated, as that would be unacceptable to your conscious mind. I.e. solid doors don't normally have a habit of vanishing before your eyes.

When you turn to where the door really should be, you will, usually, find the door there as normal. Now you may have two, or more, doors where there should only be one. If you go through the real door, you will find the rest of the house as it should be, hopefully. But, if you go through a false door, the mind knows it's false and won't accept it opening to a normal part of your house that it knows can't possibly be there. So, if you open this door you will find something else. It is usually a corridor or passage, you don't have, leading off into other parts of the house you don't have either.

From then on, if you go through this door, you are in Wonderland, where everything is possible, just not very plausible. What you are doing, in effect, is entering the astral dimension via uncontrolled creation, through this door you don't have, but now do. Once the subconscious mind starts creating like this it continues to do so at a geometric rate. It has to, for the conscious mind to assimilate the abnormal situation it is in. At some stage, in this creative maelstrom, the subconscious mind loses it completely and starts tuning in to other parts of the astral. At this point of the projection, all semblance of reality is lost and you fade into the astral dimension proper.

There are many ways this "Alice" effect can happen during a projection; the above example is just one variation. It has been noted by many projectors that at some-time during a projection they seem to lose control of it. Objects appear, disappear, and generally everything gets a little strange. This is caused, basically, by the subconscious mind's vast creative ability being triggered. It starts making and unmaking things, and tuning into other areas of the astral and generally making everything difficult for the poor projector.

To avoid the above problem: Concentrate on what you are doing while you are projecting and don't let your mind wander. The vision reversal problem can be minimised if you concentrate on your forward vision during projection, i.e., focus in one direction at a time. When you turn, follow the room around with your vision and don't allow it to flit from one view to another. The astral is not a good place to relax if you have serious plans.

The vast creative power of the subconscious can, however, be utilised. It is an extremely valuable tool if you know how to use it. I will outline ways to do this, in the third part of this series, under the heading: "Virtual Reality Projection" where I will outline how to custom create your own personal astral realm.

Melting Hands

When you project the astral body close to the physical world you do not have a body as such. But, the mind cannot accept this and so provides a thought form one made out of etheric matter. If you try and look at your body, say your hands, you will find they start to melt very quickly. They look pale and odd, and in a couple of seconds your fingers start to melt away like ice under a blow torch. They shorten into pale stumps, then the rest of your hand and arm starts to melt away too. This melting effect only seems to happen when you deliberately try and observe a body part or consciously create something.

Deliberately observing an astral body part like this, uses the conscious mind, which, having poor creative powers, can't hold complex shapes together for very long and it is this that causes the melting effect. If you happen to notice parts of your body, in passing, during projection this melting effect will not be seen.

Created Thought Form Objects

You can use your conscious mind to create objects while projecting. The duration of these, thought form, created objects depends on the strength of your creative visualisation ability. It also depends on how much time and effort you put in to a creation.

This same melting phenomena happens with any conscious creation done in the astral dimension. If you create for example, a sword, it will appear in your hand just as you imagine it, briefly, and then melt away just like the hand did. If you concentrate on it you can hold it in shape, but as soon as your concentration wavers so does the creation. This is similar to any other visualisation you do in the real world. It is difficult, and you have to concentrate to hold the visualisation in your mind's eye. Once your concentration wavers, so does the visualised image. This illustrates the vast difference between the creative powers of the conscious and the subconscious mind.

To make a lasting thought form object you have to trick the subconscious mind into creating it for you. I will deal with this subject, in greater depth, later in the series.

How Does Projection Happen?

During sleep, the energy body, also known as the etheric body or vitality sheath, is put on charge. It expands and opens in order to accumulate and store energy. The energy body can, normally, only do this in its expanded state during sleep. Once expanded, the chakras trickle power, in the form of etheric matter, into the energy body. During this recharging process the astral body separates and tunes into the astral dimension where it can create and experience dreams.

If this separation is done consciously, or if you become aware after it, you can take some control over it. It then becomes an OOBE, astral projection or lucid dream. The main differences between an OOBE, astral projection and a lucid dream are:

The OOBE

The OOBE (out of body experience) is a real time projection close to the physical world. This often occurs as part of a near death experience. This is where a person is knocked out of their body as a result of some kind of severe trauma, i.e. car accident, surgery, heart attack, child birth etc.

OOBE'ers are aware of things happening in the real world, in real time; such as conversations and events centred around, or near to, their physical body.

In many cases, these events and conversations are accurately reported by the person after they have returned to their body.

Note: The OOBE is slightly different from astral projection or lucid dreaming because of its real time, objective aspect. This is caused by the astral body containing a large amount of etheric matter, which holds it close to the physical world.

There are two main causes of real time OOBE:

1. A person's body is near death, or thinks it is, which causes a large amount of etheric matter to be channelled into the astral body in preparation for the death process.

2. The person has active chakras which are doing a similar thing, i.e. channelling etheric matter into the astral body. Having active chakras can be a natural ability, or it can be developed by training.

Note: You can project consciously, and have a real time OOBE if enough etheric matter is generated by the chakras. In an OOBE, reality is perceived as objective (real) and time is normal (real time).

Technically, when you project into the physical world in real time as in an OOBE, it is really into the boundary area of the buffer zone, between the physical and astral dimensions. If the astral body contains enough etheric matter it can exist only slightly out of phase from reality. This means the projection is in real time and so close to the physical dimension as to be indistinguishable from it. Note: I have checked this many times, by projecting, in real time, during the day and scouting my local area for road works, accidents, incidents etc., then verifying the accuracy of my findings afterwards.

There are strong natural barriers to conscious, real time projection, the OOBE, in the physical world. The amount of etheric matter generated and channelled to the astral body, is one of them. It limits the duration of any real time projection to the degree of chakra development and control.

The Astral Projection

This is where the astral body is projected into the astral dimension, where things are quite different from the real world. Time is distorted and extended, i.e., an hour in the astral can be like a few minutes in the physical dimension, depending on what part of the astral you are in. Reality is fluid and changeable.

The Lucid Dream

This is where a person becomes fully aware that they are

dreaming during a dream. They either take some kind of conscious control over the course of events, or they convert the experience into an astral projection. Lucid dreaming is more similar to an astral projection than to an OOBE, as time and reality are distorted.

Astral Projection Or Lucid Dream?

Many astral projectors black out before making a conscious exit from their body and return to awareness in the astral dimension. You become aware after the actual separation from the physical body and are usually already in the astral dimension. If you miss the conscious exit from your body you are technically having a lucid dream, not an astral projection as you have become aware after separation.

All three types of projection are closely related, i.e., they all involve the astral body separating from the physical and experiencing a reality separate from the physical body.

Chapter 2

STARTING OUT

Starting Out

After the physical body has fallen asleep, the astral body always projects into the physical world. Once the energy body has expanded, the astral body floats free and hovers just above the physical body, but within the expanded energy body's field of influence. Within this field, known as cord activity range, the astral body is held close to the physical world as it is within a field of etheric matter. During a conscious astral projection it may appear as if you are projecting straight into an astral plane. But there is always an intermediary phase at the beginning, when you are existing as an astral form close to the physical dimension. This, real time part of any projection, may be missed if you black out at the moment of projection. The area around the body, within cord activity range, is flooded with etheric matter and within this field the astral body is held in real time close to the physical dimension.

Etheric Matter

Etheric matter is the actual life force substance generated by all living things by simply being alive. It is a substance in-between physical matter and astral matter, part physical and part astral. This etheric matter has actual weight. It is a very refined substance in between matter and energy and is similar to its coarser cousin, ectoplasm. There have been scientific studies done on this phenomena. Dying people in hospitals have had their beds placed on delicate scales shortly before death and hooked up to EEG and ECG monitors. In all cases, at the exact moment of death, a sudden weight loss of approximately one quarter of an ounce is observed. This is caused by a large amount of etheric matter being transferred into the astral body at the moment of physical death. This is similar to the sudden transfer of etheric matter into the astral body during a near death experience where the body believes it is dying. This sudden, massive transfer of etheric matter is the start of the death process.

Ectoplasm

Ectoplasm has been studied in a similar fashion. Materialisation mediums have been placed on delica-

te scales and then asked to produced ectoplasm onto another set of fine scales. These mediums were observed to lose weight at exactly the same rate as the weighed ectoplasm gained weight.

When the medium reabsorbed the ectoplasm this weight transfer was reversed.

Ectoplasm is produced by the chakras. It converts part of the physical mass of the mediums body into another substance, ectoplasm.

Interdimensional Manifestation

Any non-physical or disincarnate entity, including the astral body, in order to function, in real time, close to the physical dimension; must contain etheric matter.

Without etheric matter, non-physical entities fade back into their dimension of origin. Etheric matter can only be obtained from living inhabitants of the physical world.

Energy Flow

The famed "Silver Cord" does more than just tie the two bodies together. It is a true umbilical cord, transmitting information and energy between the physical and subtle bodies. It is seen by some projectors and not seen by others. Sometimes it is seen emanating from the navel, sometimes from the forehead. The area the cord is seen emanating from may depend on chakra activity. Whichever chakra is the strongest, most active, could have control of energy flow to the subtle bodies. There is also the belief system of the projector to consider and the creative power of the subconscious mind. The cord will usually appear to be wherever you believe it will be, courtesy of the subconscious.

Once the astral body enters the astral dimension it must have a good supply of astral energy from the chakras in order to interact strongly with that dimension. Clear astral memory depends greatly on the amount of energy available. As the astral dimension is the natural domain of the astral body, it will not fade out of it due to a lack of energy. As in the real world, if a person hasn't eaten or slept for a few days they don't dissolve into another dimension. They just get weak and listless and don't interact strongly with the physical world.

What it boils down to is this: The astral mind must have enough energy to give it strong, vivid memories. These astral memories must be strong enough to make a good

*sized wrinkle in the physical brain, so the physical mind
can recall them when it wakes up.*

*For example, if you haven't slept for a few days you will
be tired, listless and your interaction with reality will
be weak and vague. If you see a movie in this tired state
you will retain little memory of it. Afterwards, you may
only remember fragments of it and your memory of it
will be a vague blur. If however, you see a movie when
you are well rested, fresh and full of energy, it is different. You take in everything about the movie and enjoy
it. Your memory of it will be crystal clear.*

*This is similar to what happens after a low powered
astral journey. The astral body lacks energy and so does
not have clear enough impressions of its journey. This
causes it to fail making its memories the dominant ones
when it returns return to the physical body. As I stated
earlier, there must be strong, vivid memories if a wrinkle
is to be made in the physical brain and the experience
remembered.*

Chakras Use

*Fully developing the chakras and learning how to control
them can take many years, depending on natural ability.*

This will not, however, stop you using them in a very basic way; to enhance your OOBE's and lucid dreams, at a very early stage in your development. Raising energy and stimulating the chakras is extremely simple to do. This raised energy will automatically flow into your astral body, prior to and during projection.

By learning to raise energy and control the flow of power through the chakras, the nature of your dreams, lucid dreams and OOBE's will change.

They will become vivid and unforgettable experiences. This, in a way, gives you a second life, full of rich experiences you can enjoy, learn and grow from.

Higher Levels And Their Buffer Zones
The commonly accepted names for the seven known levels of existence, from lowest to highest, are: Physical, Astral, Mental, Buddhic, Atmic, Anupadaka and Adi. These higher planes are similar in structure to the astral dimension but at a much higher level of consciousness and are completely separate from it. In between the different levels are intermediary areas or buffer zones, sometimes called lower sub planes.

A good analogy for the different dimensions and their buffer zones is the Earth's atmosphere: if the air in the Earth's atmosphere was the astral dimension, the stratosphere would be the buffer zone and the vacuum of space would be the mental dimension. You can fly in the Earth's atmosphere in a normal air plane/astral body. A very powerful jet plane is needed to take you into the stratosphere, but you need a space ship/mental body, to travel through space. This explains why a different subtle body is needed to travel into these different levels of existence.

The astral body can enter the buffer zones, or sub planes, of the dimensions above and below the astral dimension, if it contains the correct type of energy. I.e. To exist in the buffer zone between the physical/astral levels (in real time) the astral body must contain etheric energy. To exist in the buffer zone between the astral/mental levels it must contain mental energy.

Higher Level Projection

With enough control over the chakras, the energy for these higher levels can be produced. The production of one particular type of energy will raise the consciousness to that level and energise the corresponding subtle body. This is usually done by consciousness raising meditation and advanced energy work on the chakras. The consciousness can then experience that level of existence. If enough energy is available, and conditions are right, the meditator can project that particular subtle body directly into its natural dimension.

Depending on the skill and natural ability of the operator, if a higher body is energised and projected so, usually, are the lower ones. The astral body contains within it all the other subtle bodies and can, during a projection, project the mental body into the mental dimension and so on. This will sometimes give multiple sets of memories from the one projection. The general rule is, whichever subtle body contains the greatest amount of energy, will have the strongest memories. These dominant memories will be the ones retained by the physical mind upon its return to the waking state.

Projecting consciously into levels higher than the astral dimension takes a high level of skill. You need to be proficient in both consciousness raising and chakra control, but it is achievable. I have, so far, projected into the

Astral, Mental, Buddhic and Atmic levels of existence. It is commonly believed that it is only possible for a human to project into the Astral, Mental and Buddhic levels and not possible to project into the higher Adi and Anupadaka.

These dimensions have been named, and are described, so someone must have been there or they would be unknown. If you realise the true nature of the mind you will understand there are no limits. It was also once said that the sound barrier would never be broken.

BTW: These dimensions don't have signposts on them saying Welcome to the Astral dimension, ta...daa! or "Mental dimension, watch your mind!". So I will describe the higher levels I have been to using these accepted names.

The Astral Dimension

This is a topsy-turvy world like Alice found in Wonderland. Everything seems objective (real) but is changeable and fluid. Anything and everything can be found there, from base, coarse levels full of sexual energy; to beautiful, serene places full of spiritual harmony. Time is distorted and extended there. An hour in the Astral can seem like only a few minutes here in the physical. Compared to the physical world it is at a much higher vibration. It's like playing a video tape at twenty time's normal speed, although this is not apparent when you are there.

Moving amongst the astral dream pools is usually a hit or miss affair for most projectors. It takes a lot of experience to make planned astral journeys to specific realities.

There are an infinite number of realities, planes, realms and dream pools in this dimension. As I stated before, they naturally strata and settle into pools of related thought. During sleep, or in a lucid dream, the subconscious mind usually creates one especially for you, your own personal dream theatre.

When you become aware during a dream, you take control over it. This control is taken over from the powerful subconscious mind. Without its powerful controlling influence, your personal custom created realm will change. You will begin tuning into other sympathetic *parts of the astral, and the reality you are in will mix with other realities and take on different aspects.*

In a conscious projection into the astral dimension, you can tune into any part of it and travel into different realities, other dream pools, or a mix of many. There are various techniques for this but they all involve some way to disorient the subconscious mind, tricking it into moving you into a different Astral reality. Some projectors look at their hands and watch them melt.

Others spin around, causing left right reversals. These methods all disorient the mind and trick the subconscious into tuning into another part of the astral. It's very difficult to describe how to move amongst the levels, you really have to learn by doing it, by trial and error. You have to learn how to use and control the subconscious mind, how to trick it for a specific result.

Virtual Reality Projection

Here is a simple, reliable method, I have developed, to create your own personal realm: Get a poster of a pleasant scene, something bright and sunny. The bigger the better, but standard poster size will do. Hang it on the wall of the room you are going to project in, or another room close by. Get a small spotlight and set it so the poster is highlighted when the main light is turned off, a normal directional bedside lamp will do. Place the light under, or above, so the light spreads out over it giving a diffused effect illuminating it, a bit like a movie screen. Entering your custom realm: When you project, go towards the poster, keeping your mind blank. Don't think about what you are doing, just gaze at it and move towards it. As you approach it in this way, your subconscious mind will be tricked into creating an astral realm exactly like the poster. Just move up to and into the poster. It is like stepping into another world. Everything in this world will be exactly like in the poster. It will appear to be a normal three dimensional world, an exact copy, indistinguishable from reality.

To customise this world: Cut and paste small pictures of things, or people, you want to find in this world with you when you enter it. Don't just stick a whole picture on the poster. Get scissors and cut around the object, or person. Try and find pictures that are approximately the same scale as the poster. if you cut out a small picture of someone, living or dead, your subconscious will create a

thought form shell of them and they will be there wai-
ting for you. This may be an excellent way of communi-
cating with those that have died.

Spirit Communication: (I have a theory) the subconscio-
us creates this thought form shell of a person.

This shell can be animated by the perfect, detailed
memory of your subconscious. But, if there is love there,
between the projector and this created person, the spirit
of this, deceased person, will be drawn to this scenario
and will use this opportunity to communicate with the
projector, by animating the created image of their body.

The Akashic Records

These are found in the buffer zone between the astral
and mental worlds, part astral part mental and, in a
way, extending into all levels. They are a record of every
thought and event that has ever occurred, like a huge,
infinite, mental history, picture book. The Akashic
records also contain probabilities stemming from, and
created by, past events, actions and thoughts. This is like
looking into the future. To make any kind of sense of
the Akashic records yourself, some skill in clairvoyance
is a definite help.

If you tune into the Akashic records yourself you will normally see those events with the greatest amount energy around them. Wars and disasters are the easiest to see because of this. The energy surrounding these events make them stand out above all the rest, making them easier to see. If you look into the future, the area of probabilities, you enter into a confusing maelstrom of symbolism mixed with actual events.

This future symbolism is caused by the belief systems of the major religions.

Millions of people in the world have believed in some form of prophecy for thousands of years. Whether it is the Bible's "Book of Revelations" or the prophecies of Nostradamus. These ancient prophecies are all richly steeped in symbolism. This symbolism affects the way people think and dream about the future. This symbolism, in turn, manifests in the Akashic records as symbolic representations of future events. The symbolism is a big help, it makes consulting the Akashic records easier. You can use the Akashic symbolism as an index. For example, the reference below to "The Dogs of War" is easily understandable as representing war.

The "Grim Reaper" is a universal symbol of death and destruction.

So, if you are interested in this kind of future event you tune into this symbolic index for WAR, then browse through the category of past and future wars. Apart from some clairvoyant ability, a knowledge of history, geography, religious symbolism, current affairs world leaders and heads of state is a big help; when indexing past and future events.

For example, in the future vision I give below: If I had known WHO the well known person I saw addressing a crowd below WAS, and recognised the country; I could have made an accurate prediction of future events instead of being wise, AFTER the event.

I entered the state of consciousness called the Akashic records. There I was inundated with a mass of symbolism. I was seeing in four dimensions at once. My conscious mind did not assimilate this very well. I saw wars, famines, plagues, disasters, earthquakes, volcanoes erupting, plane crashes, murders, etc., it was terribly confusing and depressing.

I saw one piece of symbolism I recognised though and tuned into it, indexed it. The Grim Reaper holding The Dogs of War (as described by various prophets) These dogs were fearsome beasts with Red eyes and slavering jaws. They were held in check by this hooded figure, with an evil skull for a face, carrying a sickle. He released these dogs as I watched, symbolising a coming war.

Tuning into this scene, I was there floating above it all, I could feel the sunshine and smell the city below me. I saw a man standing on a raised dais, under two giant scimitar swords. He was giving a charismatic speech to many thousands of people. One of the swords turned into a Christian Crusader's broad sword. The man was Saddam Hussein, the scene was in Baghdad, at the monument to the unknown soldier. I saw this six months before the Gulf war started. I did not learn WHO Saddam Hussein WAS, or WHERE this scene took place though, until it was televised during the gulf war.

Looking through the Akashic records is like leafing through an infinite mental photo album. You are bombarded with an awesome array of the sights and sounds of past, present and probable futures. You have to select

one of these thought records, tune into it and enter it.
You will then live through the record as if you were
really there, watching it as it happens.

Consulting with the Akashic records can be done alone
if you have the skill, but is normally done with the
assistance of an advanced being from a higher level of
existence. This is done as a sort of telepathic guided tour.
The enormous amount of information and chaff is fil-
tered out for you and the selected record, of past events
or future probability, is presented to you clairvoyantly,
via a telepathic link with the... librarian. Some people
claim to have entered the Akashic Records and found
something like a library there, with real books. The past,
present and future was recorded as text in these books.
Some people even say they have read a record, then
entered into it, and experience the record first hand. All
these claims are consistent with the Akashic Records.
These are librarian assisted guided tours, where the
Akashic Records have been presented as something
familiar, easy to use and easy to accept.

The Mental Dimension
This is a spectacular dimension! Iridescent rivers of

sound bounded by rainbow shores of pulsating light. Thoughts appear as kaleidoscopic patterns of light and sound. You walk across fields of ideas under a sparkling crystal sky of inspiration. If you enter this world don't try to rationalise or understand it, or you may go mad, for it is beyond human understanding.

Just accept it all, go with the flow and enjoy it!

This dimension is what, I believe, the ancient Vikings called the famed "Rainbow Bridge" into Asgard. It truly looks and feels as if you are walking up a rainbow into some wonderful world where the Gods must surely dwell.

Exist here in wondrous amazement. Let loose the child within you to play in this fairy wonderland. Everything feels real and solid. Time is even further distorted here than in the Astral and reality is kaleidoscopic.

Buddhic Dimension

This is a warm, abstract world filled with utter peace and infinite love. It is a dimension of pure White. There is no sight or sound perception here other than the all pervading, brilliant White. In this dimension you very quickly relinquish conscious thought and individuality. You cannot think for long once you enter here and there is no need or desire to do so. There is an irresistible urge drawing you into a quiet stillness. It is like being immersed in warm, pure White cotton wool. In this world you cease to be an individual and you become, PART OF THE ONE. You also cease to be male or female. In a way this is like returning to the Mother's womb. You are surrounded, absorbed and assimilated by infinite loving warmth, understanding, forgiveness and atonement.

AT-ONE-MENT.

Time here ceases to have any meaning. If you enter this world you will never, ever want to leave it, you cannot leave it, until your physical body calls and drags you back. This is the healing, resting place of the soul.

Atmic Dimension

This dimension appears be the spirit world. Here, spirits wait for those they loved during their time on earth. This is the happy place of the gathering. It is the place where the reunion of souls takes place.

The light in this world is purest, brightest silver, brighter than the flash of an arc welder. It is so bright it seems impossible to look at, but it is, for all that, a supremely gentle light, soft and soothing. It is the light of divine love. The people here appear as they did in the physical world, but at their most magnificent. They glow ecstatically, ablaze with the brightest love, happiness and joy imaginable. The atmosphere is electric and vital, but at the same time deeply spiritual. In this world you can FEEL the presence of God as a tangible all pervading force.

Communication here, is done by high level telepathic imaging, similar to one on-one clairvoyance only much more vivid and real. It leaves speech and thought for dead. Time stands utterly still here. Reality is more real and solid than normal reality. Compared to this, the physical world is a vague, tired dream full of half dead people.

I have entered this dimension only four times in my life. Each time from the very deepest consciousness raising meditation, with all my chakras wide open and fully functioning. There was also extreme crown chakra activity.

The feeling of this was like a thousand fingers vibrating, and deeply massaging, the whole top of my head above the hairline.

On these four occasions my energy has soared to seemingly impossible heights within me, carrying my spirit and consciousness with it. At the climax of this deeply mystical experience I have heard the sound of one long, pure musical note slowly rising in pitch. I have felt this note in the core of my being, in my heart, calling me, drawing me to it.

I have focused on this note and attuned to it. With every ounce of strength and energy I possessed I have focussed my consciousness on it and projected to it. Stripping away my physical body, I have projected straight into this dimension. It was just like stepping, slipping, through a heavy curtain into another place and another world. I am still aware of my physical body, duality, during this whole experience.

I look about me with wonder, the light is so silver and bright it burns deeply into my soul and I can feel its healing touch within me. There in front of me is my long dead son. He was eight years old when he left me, and he looked just as he did when I last saw him. He was beaming with happiness, his eyes bright and shining. I cuddled him up to me and wept with the joy of seeing him. I looked beyond him and there was a large crowd of people waiting for me. These were all the friends and family I had known and loved and lost during my life. There were also many people I did not know. They all seemed very familiar though and I felt I loved them all. They were clapping and jumping up and down, cheering me in greeting. There were many tears of joy and lots of hugging and kissing.

Looking beyond them, I see we are in a natural stone amphitheatre. The ground is smooth rock and it rises to a ridge a couple of hundred meters away that curves towards us. On the top of this ridge are Angels. They looked just like Michelangelo painted them. They were incredibly beautiful, with large White feathered wings, curly Golden hair and Alabaster skin. They were blowing long sparkling golden horns, and the pure high note came from them.

Stepping from the crowd I walked into the open. I look in awe at these angels and wave at them. The note *started to die away as I did this and the Angels began lowering their horns. I stand for a timeless moment in silence, looking all around me. Then everything began to shimmer and I slipped, fell back into my physical body. I wept. I have never wanted to come back.*

Death

When you leave your body for the final time, at death, this is what I believe will happen:

You will be projecting, in real time, for the first few days, close to the physical world, until your supply of etheric matter runs out. Then you will go through the second death and enter the Astral dimension. There, you will purge yourself of all desire, by being able to have anything you have ever wanted, in abundance. This is done through having the full use of your subconscious mind's powerful creative ability. Here you can saturate your every need and desire, until you see these desires for the illusions they really are.

You will then shed your Astral (desire body) and enter the Mental dimension. There you will see your past life, examine and express every thought you have ever had and every action you have ever done. There, your thoughts, memories and experiences will be added to the Akashic Record. Which is the recorded experience of the entire human existence in the physical dimension. Shedding your mental body you will then enter the Buddhic dimension.

There you will stay for timeless healing, for rest, atonement, forgiveness and understanding of self. In this world your inner wounds will heal and your soul will be nurtured by divine love. Your spirit will become whole and perfect once more. Then you will shed your Buddhic body and enter the Atmic dimension. There you will wait in the divine presence for those you love. Then, one day, you will go on to the next level of existence; where the last great mystery of life will be revealed to you....

Chapter 3
PROJECTION TRAINING

Projection Training

To trigger the projection of the Astral body, while fully conscious, there are four major requirements:

1. Relaxing your body 100% while staying awake.

2. Concentrating 100% on what you are doing.

3. Having enough energy available.

4. Pressuring the astral body to separate.

Together, these four things will trigger an OOBE.

Below are exercises that will teach how to relax the body, concentrate, clear the mind, raise energy, stimulate the chakras and enter the trance state.

Calming The Mind Relaxation

You must learn and master, a full body relaxation exercise. If you know one already it can be adapted to suit. Here is a very simple one:

Sit, or lie down, and relax. Starting with the feet, tense and relax them.

Continue this with calves, thighs, hips, stomach, chest, arms, neck and face until your whole body is deeply relaxed. Go over this a few times, making sure your muscles stay relaxed.

Note: Deep physical relaxation is the key to bringing on the trance state, i.e., deep relaxation CAUSES the trance state. Once you are in the trance state, projection on the astral body is relatively easy.

Contemplation

When you begin meditation, you will be plagued with thoughts from your surface mind, which acts like a huge Memo pad. It carries messages, reminders, pressing thoughts, problems to solve, unresolved issues etc. it is constantly busy, it NEVER rests, thoughts, thoughts, thoughts, one after the other, all clamouring for attention.

Before you attempt to clear your mind, with the breath awareness exercise below, it is wise to deal with these

surface thoughts by the act of contemplating them.
Sit comfortably, do the relaxation exercise and think,
nothing more, just think. Search out the strongest
thoughts in your mind and examine them, try to resolve
and understand them.

Note the word: Thinking. Contemplation does not invol-
ve clearing the mind, or visualisation. It requires you to
Think, deeply and thoroughly, about something, to gain
a deeper understanding of its nature and how it relates
to you, an insight.

Breath Awareness Meditation
This is a simple form of meditation. It will clear your
mind and focus your awareness.

Sit or lie down, close your eyes, do the relaxation ex-
ercise and clear your mind. Breathe deeply and slowly
and focus on the breath entering and leaving your body.
Feel it coming in and feel it going out. Focus your whole
attention on your lungs and the breathing process.
This simple action is enough to occupy your surface
mind-Firmly push intruding thoughts away, as they
begin, before they can gather strength and distract you.

Breath awareness occupies the surface mind and allows you to think on a much deeper level.

Surface Thoughts

Sounds are very distracting, they generate surface thoughts. A car horn will generate: "Who's that, what's happening?" A door opening will generate:

"Who's coming in or going out?" The surface mind is always very curious about what is happening around you. It wants to know all, and it wants to inform you of every little thing going on around you. It will pressure you to open your eyes, get up and go find out what's happening.

Don't allow this to happen. USE these annoying, attention getting thoughts as a training aide. By learning to quash and ignore them, your powers of concentration will grow. Stop these annoying little thoughts as they begin, before they can take root and grow into something stronger.

For example:

Who's that, what's happening? becomes: *"Who's th............ "*

Who's coming in, or going out? becomes: *"Who's co............ "*

With practise the start of these distracting thoughts will get shorter and shorter until you get:

Wh....?........?..........and " W...?...................."

And finally:
........?.........?.............................?...................

Many people say they can't clear their mind as they are too easily distracted by all the small noises that sur-round them, in normal day to day activity.

DON'T use music or other sounds to blanket these out, USE them for training. It's like weight lifting, if you train with feather dusters your strength will not increase. You need to master this, the hard way, if you want to give your mind real muscle.

Slowly but surely you will master the ability to clear your mind. Once accomplished, you will have gained a valuable mental tool. You will be able to concentrate 100% of your attention, on one task, to the TOTAL exclusion of everything else.

I sometimes meditate, in the trance state, successfully, in a noisy, crowded room with little children crawling all over me. NOTHING breaks my concentration.

Concentration

You must be able to concentrate and focus completely on what you are doing. Lack of concentration is the single, biggest cause of projection failure. It affects every aspect of projection, from the relaxation exercise, to the trance state and actual projection.

To test your ability to concentrate: Sit and relax. Close your eyes and clear your mind of ALL thought. Breath slowly and deeply and count each breath, at the end of each exhale. Hold it totally BLANK, apart from the counting,

for as long as you can. See how long you can hold it like

this. Be honest with yourself every time a thought intrudes start counting from the beginning again.

You are doing well if can do this for longer than ten breaths. Ten breaths is, however, not long enough. Don't worry though, this can be improved on with the exercises below.

Concentration Exercise (1)

After image retention: Relax, calm your mind, and look at a candle or a light bulb. Place this light in front of you, a couple of feet away, and stare fixedly at it for a minute or two. Close your eyes and concentrate on the after image this will generate behind your closed eyelids. Try and keep sight of it for as long as possible. Use breath awareness to keep the mind clear, while you are doing this. Try and make the after image grow, instead of fading away.

Concentration Exercise (2)

One point stare: Pick a spot on a wall and gaze at it. Don't focus on it, just gaze at it gently. Clear your mind of ALL thoughts and forcibly hold it blank. Concentrate HARD, on breath awareness while you are doing this.

When you feel a thought beginning, push it away, don't let it finish! Hold this for as long as you can. Do this several times a day, or more if you can.

Concentration Exercise (3)

Energy breathing: Sit and relax. Close your eyes and clear your mind. Do the breath awareness exercise and imagine the air you are breathing in is brightly coloured energy of your favourite colour. Imagine the air you are breathing OUT is a murky Grey, full of toxic waste. This is a purification exercise. It stimulates your chakras into absorbing energy on the inhale and getting rid of negati-ve energy on the exhale.

Note: Try your best not to tense up while you are doing these concentration exercises, it is ALL mental. in the beginning, it may feel as if you have to tense your mind into a tight ball to stop it thinking, but in time you will find the opposite to be true. When you get used to it, clearing the mind is VERY relaxing.

The Trance State

When you have attained a deep level of relaxation and mental calmness, you will feel your body begin to get very, very heavy. This heaviness is the main symptom of your brain waves changing from the Beta to the Alpha level as you enter a trance. The trance state is caused by deep physical and mental relaxation. There is nothing weird or supernatural about it. It simply means your body has entered the sleep state while your conscious mind is fully awake.

How To Enter A Trance

Do the relaxation exercise and calm your mind through breath awareness. Imagine you are climbing down a ladder in the dark. Don't visualise a ladder, just imagine you can feel yourself doing it. On the exhale, feel yourself climbing a step or two down the ladder with your imaginary Hands (outlined below). On the inhale, feel yourself holding still on the ladder. What is needed is a mental falling effect inside your mind. This changes the level of brain wave activity from the awake level (Beta) to the asleep level (Alpha) or the deep sleep level (Theta). Once your level of brain wave activity reaches Alpha you will enter a trance. Keep doing this for as long as it takes. The time it takes to enter trance will vary, depending on your experience with deep relaxation and mental calmness.

Note: Once you get the heavy feeling, stop the mental falling exercise.

If you don't like the ladder, imagine you are in a lift, feel yourself falling on the exhale and holding on the inhale. Or, imagine you are a feather, feel yourself floating down on the exhale and holding still on the inhale. As I stated above, you need a mental falling effect to lower your level of brain wave activity. This mental falling effect, when combined with deep relaxation and mental calmness, will cause you to enter the trance state.

Feel free to use any scenario you are familiar with to bring about this going deeper feeling.

A trance feels like: Everything gets quieter and you feel like you are in a much bigger place. There is a very slight humming feeling in your body.

Everything feels different. It feels a bit like putting a cardboard box over your head in the dark, you can feel the atmosphere change. It's like everything goes fuzzy or slightly blurred. Any sharp noises, while in trance, feel like a physical blow to the Solar Plexus.

Deep Trance

The level of trance you achieve depends greatly on your relaxation, concentration skills and will power. To enter a deeper trance, i.e., Theta level and beyond, you have to concentrate much more and for much longer, on the mental falling sensation aided by breath awareness. The first level of trance, i.e., when you get very heavy, is quite deep enough for projection. I strongly advise against forcing yourself deeper than a light trance, until you have plenty of experience with the trance state.

How can you tell if you are entering a deep trance? There are four very noticeable symptoms:

1. An uncomfortable feeling of cold that doesn't make you shiver, coupled with a steady loss of body heat.

2. Mentally, you will feel very odd and everything will feel extremely slooooow. Your thought processes will slow down as if you had been given a strong pain killing injection.

3. You will feel disassociated from your body, i.e., a strong floating sensation and everything will seem far away.

4. Total physical Paralysis.

Note: These four things, ALL TOGETHER, signify you are entering a deep trance.

Do not mistake the mild floating sensation you sometimes get with light trance, i.e., as you astral body comes loose. Or the slight loss of body heat from sitting still for a long time and the mild paralysis, i.e., the heaviness, for a deep trance. The sensation of deep trance is quite uncomfortable and unmistakable for what it is. It is very difficult to get into the deep trance state, as you need highly developed relaxation, concentration and trance state skills plus lots and lots of will power and mental energy. You will not accidentally fall into it.

If you are worried you are going too deep, remember this:

You CAN pull yourself out of it at any time. Concentrate ALL your will on moving your fingers or toes. Once you can move a finger or toe, flex your hands, move your arms, shake your head, i.e., reanimate your body; and get up and walk around for a few minutes. Falling into a deep trance should not be a problem with these exercises.

I have seen many people in meditation groups etc., enter a light trance and not be able to pull themselves out of it, i.e., they float away with the faeries.

Usually some kind person will talk them out of it or massage their wrists etc.

to get them to come back to reality. This is unnecessary and is the result of lop- sided training, i.e., no concentration or will power training. The person only THINKS they cannot come back and therefore does not try very hard. It is also a good way of getting attention from the group.

Note: Your mind is extremely powerful and has vast untapped resources. It can do ANYTHING, no limits, if it is trained, conditioned and properly motivated.

Energy Body Expansion

At some point after entering the trance state, you will feel a mild paralysis come over you. This will soon be accompanied by a deepening vibration and a buzzing feeling all over. You may also feel like you are huge and swollen.

The paralysis, vibrations and the huge feeling are symptoms of the energy body expanding and the astral body loosening. This is part of the normal sleep process. The energy body expands and opens in order to accumulate and store energy. During this, the astral body drifts free, slightly out phase with the physical body.

Trance Familiarity

Many people blow their projection simply because they are not used to the trance state. They think it is a briefly opened window into the Astral dimension. This is simply NOT true. If you stay mentally and physically calm when you enter the trance state, you can maintain it for hours. I regularly spend several hours at a time in the trance state, during meditation.

If, when you enter trance, you think: "Yes! I've done it!...I'm in a trance!

Gotta hurry and get out quick...before it stops!" You'll blow it for sure! The trance will be ended by the simple act of getting over excited, i.e., breaking relaxation and mental calmness. It's a good idea to spend time in the trance state, just getting used to it, before you try and project. Just relax, stay calm, focus on breath awareness,

*and hold the trance. It won't end until you want it to.
Get used to how it feels.*

*When you are comfortable doing this, do the energy rai-
sing and chakra stimulation exercises, below, in trance.*

Note:

*1. You do not HAVE to be in a trance to learn energy
and chakra work, it just works better in trance.*

*2. Trance practise can be done lying down, but is best
done in a comfortable arm chair.*

*Your astral body will be loose in the trance state, so try
lifting your astral arms and legs out, one at a time. Use
your HANDS to do this, as shown in the next section.
Focus and FEEL your awareness in an arm and slowly
lift it free of your body. You may feel a slight tickling
or localised dizziness inside your arm or leg, as you do
this. Lift your astral arm up and look at it, with your
eyes closed, but DON'T move a muscle. In this state you
should be able to see it through your closed eyelids, but
don't worry if you can't, this will come later.*

Lifting your astral arms free is good practise for projection. Later, you will use these astral arms to pull your astral body free of the physical.

Tactile imaging

Tactile imaging is a perception or Feeling of localised bodily awareness.

Your hands are very closely linked to your bodily awareness. They are intimately aware of every part of your body. Imaginary HANDS, outlined below, is only an extension of this (hand to body) awareness. When you are asked to feel your awareness, in any part of your body, PRETEND your hands, your real hands, are going to touch that area of your body. Then use the awareness this generates in that area to imagine your imaginary HANDS are there.

Keep your eyes closed and hold your hands out a foot or so in front of your face. Concentrate, FEEL where they are and try and SEE them through the blackness behind your closed eyes. Cross your wrists, slowly move them about, turn your hands over, open and close your fingers. Look hard, concentrate, as if you were trying to see *in the dark, and you will see a faint moving shadow in your mind's eye, where your hands and arms are.*

Close your eyes and touch the tip of your nose with the index finger of your right hand. You'll find you can accurately put that finger on any part of your body with your eyes closed. Try it; put your hand, your real hand, on different parts of your body like this. You know exactly where your hands are at all times, you can sense and feel where they are. If you observe what is happening in your mind, while you are doing this, you will notice you become aware of the part of your body you are going to touch, the instant you make the decision to touch it.

Go over your whole body like this, getting used to the sensation of awareness it generates in different areas of your body.

What is happening is this: Part of your mind is shifting into, and Highlighting, the area you are going to touch, in order to guide your hand to the exact spot.

Your mind shifts part of its awareness to this spot and acts like a homing beacon for your hand.

The ability to shift your awareness into different parts of your body like this is Vital to energy work and this projection method.

Note: You do not have to actually visualise these HANDS, i.e., see or imagine you can see them. It is ALL tactile, NOT visual. You just have to be able to pretend to FEEL them doing something, like you are rehearsing some simple action in your mind. I originally developed this technique for blind people.

Blind people cannot visualise AT ALL, if they have been blind since birth, but they do have a very keen sense of bodily awareness. The majority of sighted people also have great trouble with visualisation of any kind, and all projection techniques depend heavily on visualisation. This being the case, I developed a projection technique that does NOT depend on visualisation to exert pressure on the astral body to separate. It turned out to be so much easier, and more successful, than the other visualisation based techniques, that I discarded them in favour of this simple tactile method.

Note: Blind people are not blind in astral form. The

astral body does not have any organs as such; it is a point of consciousness only. The astral body you are aware of while projecting is provided courtesy of the subconscious minds creative ability.

Chapter 4

BASIC ENERGY WORK

Basic Energy Work (The Major Chakras)

The major chakras are situated at:

1. Base chakra (base of spine, between anus and genitals)

2. Spleen chakra (slightly below the belly button)

3. Solar Plexus chakra (1 hand-span above the belly button)

4. Heart chakra (centre of the chest)

5. Throat chakra (base of throat, above where it joins the chest)

6. Brow chakra (exact centre of forehead)

7. Crown chakra (whole top of head above the hairline)

They are best imagined as roughly the size of the palm of your hand, except for the crown chakra which is much larger.

What Are Chakras?

Chakras are non-physical organs that transform raw subtle energy into more subtle, and useable, forms of energy, of a different type. The chakras do not, themselves, contain energy. Raw energy is drawn up from the planet, by the minor chakras in the legs and feet, and fed into the main chakra system.

Subtle energy is, in essence, pure thought energy that permeates and binds the universe together. This living energy field can be tapped, more deeply, by the application of focussed, creative will. It can be drawn into the human body and transformed, by the chakra system, into a more subtle and useable form of energy.

The chakras are attached to the spinal cord and nervous system via certain glands and nerve ganglia. The full chakra system is extremely complex.

There are 7 major and over 300 minor chakras in the human body. There are also several non-physical chakras situated outside of the body. Detailed maps of the chakra system and their connecting meridians and pathways, have been used for thousands of years in Eastern mysticism and medicine, i.e., acupuncture. The *chakra system is used with every psychic ability, no exceptions. Whatever the psychic ability, the method of development or the terminology used to describe it; it is all done the same way, through chakra stimulation. It is impossible to manifest any psychic ability without first stimulating the chakras.*

Many people will deny this, above, and claim they have never done any chakra, energy work, but still have psychic abilities. There are many ways to develop yourself, agreed, but they all, directly or indirectly, stimulate the chakra system. And let's not forget natural ability.

Many people are born with naturally active chakras and hence, natural psychic ability.

Mediums are people who exhibit psychic abilities when aided by a nonphysical spirit entity. This entity stimulates the chakras of the medium directly, by melding with the medium and causing psychic abilities, clairvoyance, channelling, healing, production of ectoplasm etc. to manifest through the medium. This is why they are called Mediums or channels, i.e., they have the ability to become a passive vehicle for a spirit entity to affect, or communicate with, the physical world.

You do not need a spirit entity to develop and use a psychic ability. If you learn to control your own chakras and energy, you can do these things on your own, with no spirit entity involved, and without the inherent risk involved with that method.

Energy Raising

Sit, or lie down, do the relaxation exercise and clear you mind with breath awareness. Focus your awareness in your feet. Use your HANDS to pull energy up from your feet, through your legs, to the base chakra. Imagine you are gripping energy and pulling it up through you. Just like you did when you used these HANDS with breath awareness and colour breathing, pulling air and energy into your lungs.

Note: Try and imagine your HANDS are inside your legs and just inside the front of your torso as you do this.

Use breath awareness as an aide to energy raising. Draw energy up through you, with the inhale, and hold it in place on the exhale. Do this over and over again, pulling energy to the Base chakra, for at least a few minutes.

You may or may not feel anything while you do this. Even if you don't, you are still drawing some energy with this exercise. The amount of energy drawn up through you will increase as the chakras develop with time and use. From the feet, up the legs to the base centre, is a natural path for the energy that flows through you. This energy will stimulate your chakras and they will transform this, basic energy, into energy of a different type. This transformed energy will then flow into your subtle bodies, energising them.

With practise, you will actually FEEL this energy tingling and surging through you.

Chakra Stimulation

Opening a chakra: Your imaginary HANDS are used for this. Imagine you are tearing open a bread roll at the site of a chakra when you are asked to do this. You don't have to visualise anything, just FEEL like you are doing this, as if you were doing it in real life without looking at what you are doing.

Chakras are non-physical centres, so you need a non physical method to stimulate them. This is achieved by focusing your awareness in the area of a chakra and using your mind to manipulate it. You need a localised, mental opening effect in a chakra to stimulate it; this tearing open action, with your imaginary HANDS, provides it. By moving your point of awareness to the site of a chakra and causing a mental opening effect with your HANDS, you are directly stimulating the chakra. Note: Do the energy raising exercise, as above, before stimulating the chakras. Use breath awareness to aide your HANDS in pulling energy into each chakra, i.e., draw energy UP on the inhale and HOLD it on the exhale, with all the chakra stimulation exercises below.

1. Base chakra: Raise energy up to your Base chakra. Use your HANDS to open it. Pull energy INTO the Base chakra. Repeat this first step, thoroughly, seven times.

2. Spleen chakra: Draw energy from the feet, through the Base chakra and on up to the Spleen chakra. Open the Spleen chakra. Repeat this three times, starting at feet.

3. Solar Plexus chakra: Draw energy from the feet, through the Base and Spleen chakras and on up to the Solar Plexus chakra. Open the Solar Plexus chakra. Repeat this three times, starting at feet.

4. Heart chakra: Draw energy up from the feet, through the Base, Spleen and Solar Plexus chakras and on up to the Heart chakra. Open the Heart chakra. Repeat this three times, starting at feet.

5. Throat chakra: Draw energy up from the feet, through the Base, Spleen, Solar Plexus and heart chakras to the Throat chakra. Open the Throat chakra. Repeat this three times, starting at feet.

6. Brow chakra: Draw energy up from the feet, through the Base, Spleen, Solar Plexus, Heart and Throat chakras to the Brow chakra. Open the Brow chakra. Repeat this three times, starting at feet.

7. Crown chakra: Draw energy up to the Crown chakra as in the previous step. Open the Crown chakra. This chakra is much larger than the others (whole top of head, above hairline). Imagine you have a much larger, flatter bread roll inside the top of your head and are tearing it open with your HANDS, or like you are tearing your scalp open. Repeat this entire process twice, starting with the feet.

Note: Try your best not to tense any muscles during these exercises. You may, however, feel a slight internal contracting, a feeling that is NOT muscular while you are stimulating your chakras. These are the glands and nerve ganglia, linked to the chakras, contracting in response to the stimulation. This internal contracting is normal.

The Base, or Root chakra, is THE MOST IMPORTANT ONE TO ACTIVATE. This chakra is the doorway for the subtle energy. Unless this is opened sufficiently, the energy cannot flow into the other chakras. I suggest you concentrate most of your time and energy into stimulating your Base chakra, at least in the early stages of chakra development.

Note: When I first started raising energy and developing my chakras, many years ago, I didn't feel ANY sensation for several months. Many people, though, have reported to me strong energy and chakra sensation the first time they used them. Some people have more natural chakra activity than others. Lack of any sensation, though, will not stop you from stimulating and developing them, even if, as was my case, you feel nothing at first. I did not have ANY natural chakra activity or ANY natural psychic ability when I first started energy work.

Stop And Check

Check your muscles for any tensing during the energy raising and chakra stimulation exercises, and re-relax as needed. Your muscles will automatically try and respond to the mental action of pulling energy up through you. Remember, this is ALL mental, your body must stay calm and relaxed throughout.

Chakra Sensations

The sensations you will feel in your chakras can vary, according to the degree of activity occurring in them, i.e., your physical make up, natural ability, concentration and relaxation skills affect this. It can vary from a gentle warmth, a localised pressure, or bubbling (like stomach wind), a localised dizziness, a tingling, a gentle pulsing, to a heavier throbbing, or a combination of some or all of the above. The heavier the thrumming, the more active the chakra. If you place your hand on a chakra, when it is active, you will actually feel the flesh pulsing.

Some of the chakras, when active, can cause other odd, localised sensations:

Base chakra: You may feel a very slight burning or ting-ling, or a cramping, like you have been riding a bicycle for too long, to begin with. Once it is working properly, you will feel a gentle pulsing or throbbing between your legs, at the site of the chakra.

Solar Plexus Chakra: This can sometimes cause a short-ness of breath feeling, which can cause you to hyper-ven-tilate. This will pass, with time and use, as the chakra stabilises. Heart Chakra: The heart chakra merits special mention due to the strong, and sometimes frightening, sensation it can cause. When strongly activated it can feel like your heart is racing at an impossible rate. It is a powerful sensation. Try and ignore this when it happens, it won't hurt you. It is not your heart racing but the chakra working. I know this is easier said than done, ignoring it, but with practise and familiarity you can. This racing is more apparent in the early stages of development. I think this is caused by a lack of energy flowing from the lower centres. In a way it is like a pump racing, when it does not have enough fluid to pump.

*The heart chakra, when fully operational, feels like:
Place one hand on your chest, with your finger tips resting in the middle of it over your heart. Tap your fingers on your chest, in time with your heart. Increase this rate until you are tapping as fast and hard as your fingers can move.*

Note: Your actual heart rate does NOT speed up with this racing sensation. If you hook yourself up to a heart monitor, you will see that your heart beat hardly changes at all.

Throat Chakra: The throbbing in it can cause a very mild choking feeling, because of the sensitive area it is in. This feels something like having an emotional lump in the base of your throat.

Crown Chakra: When fully active it feels like a thousand soft, warm fingers gently massaging the inside of the top of your head, above the hairline, and extending down in the centre of the forehead, to include the brow chakra, which is part of it. This sensation is the reason the Buddhists call it "The Thousand Petalled Lotus".

Note: You may feel a stronger sensation in some chakras and little or none in others. Concentrate on the lowest ones with the least sensation. This will help balance the energy flow in the chakra system. If you are unbalanced, during projection the inactive chakras can cause failure, i.e., you may get your body partly loose but find you are stuck to your body at the site of the inactive chakra. If this happens, concentrate on stimulating the inactive chakra prior to projection.

(See also Chapter 8, Closing Energy Centres).

Psychic Abilities

After beginning chakra work, you may find psychic abilities start to grow in you. This is a natural offshoot of stimulating the chakras. In my next series, on more advanced energy work, I will show how to develop and use some of these abilities and how to raise the Kundalini.

Practise

Some relaxation, breath awareness, concentration and mental hands exercises should, ideally, be carried out daily. They can be done anywhere and anytime you have a few minutes to spare.

How Long Does It All Take?

Many people have asked me "How long does it take to learn projection?" My answer is: Because everybody has different levels of natural ability and skill, it will take as long as it takes. I have had letters from people, who have been trying various other methods for several years, but with no results; get out the very first time they tried this technique. Other people, with NO relaxation or concentration skills at all, are looking at several months training before they will get out.

Chapter 5
ASTRAL ROPE TECHNIQUE

Astral Rope

A key ingredient to the new projection techniques is an invisible, imaginary ROPE hanging from your ceiling. This ROPE will be used to exert dynamic pressure at a single point on your astral body to force its separation from the physical.

The ROPE technique is similar, but more direct and hence more effective than other more passive and indirect methods, such as reaching out and pulling vibrations into you, or visualizing yourself in front of yourself. The idea of pulling vibrations into you is vaguely illogical, if you understand the mechanics of projection.

The vibrations are an effect and NOT a cause of projection. When enough pressure is exerted on the astral body to loosen it sufficiently, the energy body expands and energy flows through the chakra system to be stored in the energy body. This flow of energy through the hundreds of chakras and their connecting web, or meri-

*dians, CAUSES these vibrations. This normally happens,
unnoticed, during sleep. Putting The Pressure On The
more passive, indirect methods of projection do exert
some pressure on the astral body to separate, but over
a wide area. They still shift the point of consciousness
out of the body, albeit obtusely. Any mental action that
exteriorizes the point of consciousness will exert some
pressure on the astral body.*

*The action of pulling yourself hand over hand up a rope
is a strong, one pointed, natural action that is easy to
imagine yourself doing. The ROPE technique concentra-
tes ALL your mental resources into one strong, DYNA-
MIC action which exerts a high level of pressure directly
on a single point of the astral body.*

*There are many other, more subtle, ways that exert pres-
sure on the astral body as well. Many of these are un-
suspected for what they are. Most meditation exercises,
for example, exert PASSIVE pressure on the astral body.
You may imagine you are going down in a lift, falling,
climbing down a ladder, or just floating downwards.
Whatever the technique, it is designed to reduce brain
activity. Any self induced, inward falling sensation pla-*

ces passive pressure on the astral body, which will cause brain activity to lower and bring on the trance state where a deeper level of the mind is revealed.

The action of inward falling obtusely shifts the consciousness out of the body, exerting passive pressure on the astral body over a wide area, but in the reverse to that needed for projection, i.e., general downwards pressure. This, in a way, is like trying to get your astral body to FALL out of your physical body on its own, i.e., your point of consciousness tries to FALL, downwards, out of the physical body.

What most people do to project is to either exert forward, passive pressure on the astral body, by visualizing themselves floating out of themselves, and HOPE, they can make it happen, i.e., trigger the projection reflex. Or, they try a more direct method, such as visualizing themselves out of their body, which is very, very, difficult. Let's face it, 99% of people can't visualize for peanuts and the act of mentally visualizing yourself OUT of your body, AND shifting your consciousness INTO this visualization is almost impossible for most people. The other popular method is to try to pull vibrations into you.

*This method is slightly more effective than most as it
exerts some pressure at a single point, but it is still an
indirect mental action and, therefore, obtuse.*

*All the above, and the general lack of information about
the mechanics of projection, i.e., HOW it happens, accounts for the extremely high failure rate amongst people
learning to project.*

*Holding passive pressure, over a wide area, on the astral
body, for long enough, WILL activate the projection
reflex, eventually. But this can take a long time and can
be mentally exhausting. I have developed, through recent
research, a better, faster and more dynamic method
of projection that is very effective. I call this technique
simply ROPE. It is not that using an imaginary rope for
projection is such a new idea, it's not, but the understanding of the mechanics of it and the application of this
knowledge to ROPE is.*

*If you fully understand how a thing works, you can
use that thing more efficiently and, therefore, get better
results.*

The new ROPE method overcomes the general misdirection of mental resources and the chronic waste of mental energy caused by the usual lengthy procedures needed for projection. ROPE shortens the time needed to cause a projection and optimizes the use of available energy.

One of the most important ingredients for a successful projection is to be properly motivated. Without this motivation you will not have enough mental energy to succeed and will either fall asleep or forget the projection afterwards. It is, therefore, important to keep preparation time as short as possible so it is not such a daunting and mentally exhausting task.

One thing a new projector has in abundance is enthusiasm. Enthusiasm is pure mental energy. ROPE, plus the understanding of HOW it works, harnesses and makes better use of this energy resource and vastly improves the success rate.

Getting The Feel Of Rope

Pin a length of ribbon, string or rope to the ceiling above you. Have it hanging within arm's reach so you can easily reach up and touch it. Reach out and touch it fre-

quently, until you are used to where it is in your mind. This ribbon is only a tactile aide. By being able to reach out and touch the ribbon, you used to the spatial coordinates of where the invisible, imaginary ROPE is. This grows both in your mind and hence as a thought form, making it easier to imagine yourself reaching out and climbing the ROPE with your imaginary HANDS.

Note: You do NOT have to actually visualize, or see, the ROPE at any time, just know where it is supposed to be. This method uses NO visualization at all.

Reaching out and pulling on this invisible, imaginary ROPE with your imaginary HANDS shifts the bodily awareness induced point of consciousness, out of the body, with a strong natural action that puts direct pressure on one point of the astral body.

Active Chakra

One important point, if you happen to have more activity in your Brow Chakra, rather than in your Heart Chakra, which is sometimes the case.

Move the position of your imaginary ROPE so your

arms would be at a degree angle above your head. If you use the visual aide, ribbon, move this so it is hanging down over your head, rather than over your chest.

Changing the angle of the ROPE shifts the point of pressure you are exerting on your astral body to the most active chakra area and gives better results.

In any case, position the angle of the ROPE at the most natural, and easy to imagine attitude for you. It is important that the angle and position of the imaginary ROPE feels natural. Experiment with this angle until it feels right for you.

Are You Ready To Project?

All the exercises in the previous parts of this series ARE necessary training for projection. They are, however, not all needed, in themselves, for the projection process. If you do all the relaxation, mental calming, mental falling, chakra opening and energy raising exercises during the actual projection, you can use up your supply of mental energy. This can cause mental exhaustion and you may find yourself short of energy and willpower for the all important exit.

All the exercises should be done separately from the projection itself. They are training and development exercises, designed to improve control over body and mind and to increase the flow of energy through the chakras. This is like working out in a gym as a part of football training. You don't actually use these exercises to play football; they just improve your fitness and strength so you are able to play football effectively.

Do the training exercises separately UNLESS you are trying for an advanced, real time projection. It is, then, still necessary to go through the full procedure, and activate all the chakras, prior to the actual projection.

The whole point of learning to project is to get your astral body to separate from the physical while fully conscious. The earlier you get a fully conscious projection the better. Otherwise, you may eventually give it all up as just too difficult. Therefore, I strongly suggest all beginners concentrate on the simplest, most effective way of getting a conscious projection. Once you have some projection experiences under your belt you can try for some of the more advanced, and hence, more difficult, types of projection.

By doing the training exercises you have learned to relax your body, to clear your mind and to concentrate. You have begun to develop (MBA) (mobile bodily aware-ness) and how to use MBA, i.e., using your imaginary HANDS to perform certain tasks both inside and out-side of your body. You have also begun to awaken and develop your chakras so your energy flow is stronger and you have, hopefully, spent time getting used to being in trance. These skills have prepared your body and mind for projection.

When To Do The Exercises

Even though the exercises, in themselves, are not all used during the projection sequence, they still need to be done regularly in order to develop the necessary skills and energy levels for conscious projection. I suggest the relaxation, concentration and mental calming exercises are done daily. Use your imaginary HANDS with these exercises. The energy, chakra work and other exercises should be done at least once a week to be effective. If you wish to do them more often, fine, just don't tire yourself out too much.

Your Projection Sequence

It is difficult to give one, universal projection sequence as everybody has different levels of skill and natural ability. For this reason I give a more flexible sequence and I suggest you tailor a projection method to fit your own needs and level of skill. Keep in mind the old saying "What works, works!" Play around with your sequence until you find what is right for you, what is easiest and most effective.

First, here is the full sequence for advanced, real time projection.

Full Sequence

Do relaxation exercises thoroughly.

1. Clear your mind through breath awareness.
2. *Enter trance using mental falling method.
3. *Raise energy and open all chakras.
4. Pull yourself out with the imaginary rope.

Note:

• Steps 3* and 4* can be swapped to suit, i.e., do the energy work before, or after, entering trance. Energy and *chakra work is more effective done in trance, but some people have trouble getting into that state. Doing the energy work first will usually help bring about the trance state.*

• IF you still have trouble getting into trance, use the ROPE climbing method at step 3 instead of the mental falling exercise, until you are in trance. Then stop the ROPE climbing and do the energy work before continuing with the projection, i.e., using the ROPE at step 3* will help force your body into the trance state.*

How To Use ROPE

This is a complete projection method in itself, if you have good powers of concentration. I suggest beginners concentrate solely on this method until they have more experience. This projection method will give you a normal Astral projection. The duration of this projection, in real time, will depend on the level of chakra development and energy flow you have attained.

1. Do the relaxation exercise thoroughly, until you are completely settled.

This should only take a few minutes, don't overdo it.

2. Reach out with your imaginary HANDS and pull yourself, hand over hand, up the strong, invisible, imaginary ROPE hanging above you. Try and imagine the feel of a strong, thick, coarse rope in your HANDS.

Don't try and visualize this ROPE! I want you to imagine you are reaching out and climbing this ROPE in the pitch dark, so you can't see it at all, you just know where it is and can imagine the feel of it. Visualization wastes valuable mental energy that can be better put to use exerting direct pressure on your astral body.

You will feel a slight dizzy sensation inside you as you do this, specifically in your upper torso. This is caused by exerting dynamic pressure on the astral body. The dizzy sensation comes from the astral body loosening. This feeling of vertigo will intensify the more you pull on the rope.

Very important Note:
1. This dizzy feeling and any feelings of pressure or vertigo, etc., caused by your mental action of pulling on the

ROPE MUST be carefully noted by you.

Learn the EXACT mental action you are doing to cause this vertigo. You will have to train your mental climbing action to cause this feeling. So, the first few times you try this ROPE method, concentrate on finding the right mental action to do this. Once you learn what it is you are doing to cause this, and can recreate it at will, you are really starting to get somewhere.

*2. Ignore *all* sensation YOU FEEL*

During Projection or it will distract you, break your concentration, and ruin your chances for projection. Concentrate on the single act of climbing your ROPE to the TOTAL exclusion of everything else. Put everything you have into this one action, but don't tense up, it must be all mental.

3. Keep climbing, hand over hand, ever upwards, and you will feel the heavy sensation come over you. The pressure you are exerting on your astral body will force you into the trance state. Ignore this when it happens and concentrate on what you are doing.

4. Keep climbing and you will feel your chakras open in response to the pressure, don't stop.

5. Next you will feel the vibrations start, your whole body will seem to be vibrating and you will feel paralysed. Concentrate, single minded, on climbing your rope, and don't stop.

6. Next you will feel yourself coming free of your body. You will buzz slightly as you pull yourself out of your body. You will exit your body in the direction of your imaginary ROPE and will be hovering above your body. You're free at last!

Note:

*A. Do *NOT* allow yourself to break concentration when the vibrations start. They are a natural EFFECT caused by energy coursing through all the hundreds of major and minor chakras in your body. If you do find yourself being distracted by this, spend more time and effort doing the concentration exercises until you overcome this problem.*

B. If you have not mastered using your imaginary HANDS for relaxation, raising energy and chakra work, you may have difficulty using them for climbing the ROPE. This does not mean you have to be able to open your chakras successfully to project using this method, you don't, it just helps if you can.

This method is very direct. It shortens the time needed to project dramatically! Once you start pulling in earnest on your ROPE you WILL enter trance, your chakras WILL open, the vibrations WILL start and you WILL project, very quickly! The speed of this method may frighten you, the first time you try it. Everything will seem to happen TOO fast. You will get used to this, though, and will appreciate having plenty of mental energy to use during your projection.

If your powers of concentration are good, you have a better chance of getting out with this method than any other, even if you haven't mastered deep relaxation and trance skills. What is needed, apart from the ability to concentrate, is the ability to carry out strong mental actions, without any corresponding muscular action, i.e., you have to be able to separate mental and physical actions.

If you have trouble with any part of the ROPE method, analyse it, find the problem area, then go back and concentrate on the related training exercises until you overcome the problem.

A ROPE Variation

Note: One good variation for the simple ROPE technique is to do the full sequence of exercises and energy, chakra work first, but separate from, the actual projection. Do the full sequence, but 'don't' close your chakras. Get up and have a break, make yourself comfortable, have a drink etc. Then return to your bed /chair fresh, spend a couple of minutes relaxing and go straight to your ROPE. This will increase the amount of chakra energy available during the projection.

The Mechanics OF How ROPE Works

ROPE is the most dynamic projection method to date and can override the need to do just about anything else, once it is learned. Let me explain a little more of the mechanics of what actually happens when you use ROPE, by breaking it down:

Clearing The Mind:

The mental act of climbing the ROPE fully occupies and clears the mind.

Brain Wave Activity:

Clearing the mind and exerting, one pointed, dynamic pressure on the astral body, forces the reduction of brain wave activity.

Deep Relaxation:

Reducing brain wave activity forces the body into a deep level of relaxation.

Trance State:

Exerting dynamic pressure on the astral body, while the physical body is deeply relaxed, and brain wave activity is at a low level, FORCES the mind and body into the trance state.

The Chakras:

Exerting dynamic pressure on the astral body, while in trance, FORCES the energy body to expand and the chakras to open.

Vibrations:

Exerting dynamic pressure on the astral body while the energy body is in its expanded state and the chakras are open causes energy to flow through the 300 odd chakras in the body and causes the vibrational state.

Separation:

Exerting dynamic pressure on the astral body while the energy body is in its expanded, vibrational state forces the astral body to separate from the physical.

Note: if you exert enough pressure on the astral body, during the final phase of the projection sequence, the exit, it will override the projection reflex completely. This forces a manual separation of the physical / astral bodies. This means: instead of involuntarily buzzing out of your body via the projection reflex, at the climax of the projection, and ending standing at the foot of your bed etc., you will exit your body in the direction you are pulling on the ROPE.

How Long Does it All Take?

The whole projection process can be done in less than fifteen minutes; I can do it in under five minutes. The speed of the method allows you to use ALL your avai-

lable energy in one burst. If you don't get out in the first fifteen minutes I doubt if you will during that attempt. If this is the case, either get up and have a break and come back to it later, or get some sleep.

Using the ROPE method, literally, amazed me with its ease and simplicity the first time I used it. It shortened my usual projection time (20-30 minutes, from a cold start) to about 5 minutes, for a normal astral projection. I still, though, use the full sequence when I do a real time projection.

My analysis of the mechanics of this process comes from using the ROPE method myself and carefully observing what was happening to my body during the separation.

My First ROPE Projection
Here is an account of the first time I tried ROPE, while I was developing it as a viable theory:

I laid down on my bed, I was thinking of my new theory. I had been working out a projection technique that blind people could do. A technique that did not require ANY optical visualization. I had come up with the idea of *using the sense of touch to exert pressure on the astral body, tactile imaging, as this sense is strongly developed in blind people.*

I lay there for a few minutes, mulling it over in my mind, while I generally relaxed and settled myself, ready for sleep. Then I decided to try it out, to see if it was practical.

Note: I did not do any of the usual relaxation, mental calming or chakra energy exercises. I just wanted to see if I could exert pressure on my astral body with this method.

I reached out my imaginary hands and began climbing the ROPE, hand over hand. I immediately felt a sensation of vertigo in my stomach and upper torso and a dizzy feeling inside my bones, like a tickling inside my arms and legs. I snapped my mind shut, stopped all thought, and focussed my will on the climbing action. I could feel the enormous pressure it was exerting on my astral body, my astral head and upper torso was starting to lift free, trying to go up the ROPE following the line of pressure I was creating.

Still pulling, I felt my brain waves drop into the alpha state and the heavy sensation came over me as I entered trance. I kept pulling and the trance deepened, my body was now paralysed. Still pulling, my chakras opened and the vibrations started. I was amazed; I had only been doing this for a couple of minutes! I kept pulling and my astral body soon buzzed free of the physical.

This was completely different from any other projection I had ever done.

The projection reflex did not seem to have time to cut in and project me out of my body. I had, literally, pulled myself free on my own. I floated above my physical body, still aware of myself on the bed. I went to go through the wall into the lounge, where there was more light, as it was pretty dark in my room. Suddenly I was in a strange world. "Where the hell am I" I thought.

There was very dim light and there was a damp fog all around me. There was a large building in front of me with an old fashioned thatched roof. To the side of me was an old rail fence made of massive, rough hewn timbers. I leaned against the fence and thought about it all.

I looked past the house and saw the reflection of water. There was a lake on the other side of the house. This didn't make any sense to me and I was getting bored, so I tried to move to another realm in the dream pool. I looked at my hand, this usually works. It was white and pale and unreal looking, it began to melt quickly, like white ice under a blowtorch. My fingers were soon stumps and then my hand melted and my arm began to follow. I tried remaking it. It grew back as I concentrated on visualizing what it should look like, but started to melt again as soon as I stopped concentrating.

Then it hit me, why this scene was so familiar to me, I was in a picture! I have a large picture hanging on the wall in my room, in the exact position where I had tried to pass through the wall. This picture has an old house with a thatched roof and a rough hewn fence around it. There is a lake behind it and it is early dawn, when the sun is just starting to illuminate things. There was no doubt about it, I was in my picture.

I'd had enough of this; it was too dim to enjoy the projection, or to do anything. I focussed on my physical body, which I could still feel. I concentrated on moving my mouth and eyes and this soon brought me back to my physical body. I sat up in bed and thought about it while I recorded the results of my experiment.

Settling back down again I tried climbing the ROPE again. Within a couple of minutes I was back out of my body again. "This is great," I thought! I hovered above my body and looked about the room. There in the gloom was the picture on the wall, the one I had entered by accident. I went towards it again, just to see if it would happen again.

As I got closer it got bigger and bigger and I seemed to shrink into it. As I got right up to it, instead of passing through it, I seemed to move into it and there I was aga-in in this dimly lit, damp world with the old house and the fence. Everything felt real about it, the fence felt like wood and even the air smelled different, it had a farm like, swampish smell about it.

Leaving the picture again and returning to my body, I again wrote everything down in my notebook. I lay there for most of the night, thinking about what had happened, mulling over the implications of it all, what it all meant....

This is how I discovered 'Virtual Reality Projection' or (VRP) This technique is, at the moment, in its infancy and only a rough method for creating a custom made world. I plan to do some more experiments with it in the near future, though, to get the bugs out of it.

Remembering it All

One of the biggest problems with any kind of conscious OOBE is remembering it all when you wake up.

Here's what you can do about this not remembering. As soon as you wake up, sit up in bed and pull those memories back. Sit up and think hard. Put aside a few minutes quiet time each morning to do this. It will train your dream memory.

During this quiet time, run key phrases through your mind until you hit on something. Say things like: I looked at my watch and... I looked at my hands and... I was walking... I was talking to... I was just going to... I was over at... I was flying over... I was having a... I was inside a... I was with... These are examples of phrases that can lead you to a fragment of dream memory you can lock on to. Make up some more phrases to suit yourself. It may feel like there is nothing in your mind to remember, but try hard and put some REAL effort into it. They are there, you just have to reach in and locate them. Once you lock onto a fragment of memory, more can be located and more and more. You will be surprised how much you can remember this way. It is important to write these down as soon as you remember them. Even if you have to do this several times during the night. They may seem vivid and unforgettable at the time but dream, or astral, memories will usually vanish in a few seconds if you don't record them. Just write down a few key words and you can fill in the blanks later. With practise, this writing down can be dispensed with as your astral recall develops.

Stuck?

Some people may find they are stuck in part of their body during projection.

They may come free of their body but be stuck at their head or stomach area. If this happens, exerting too much pressure by pulling on the rope may cause some physical pain and discomfort. There are two possible reasons for this: if you are stuck in the middle, stomach area, it may be diet related, i.e., a heavy protein or meat meal before projection can cause this.

Remedy: Eat a light meal, eat plenty but have fish or white meat instead of red meat and avoid fats, oils, nuts and cheese.

If you are stuck at the head, or some other part, this is a sign of an inactive chakra, possibly caused by an energy blockage.

Remedy: Concentrate on opening this stuck chakra during the energy exercises. If this happens during your projection sequence, stop everything and open that chakra, you will be in trance so it will be easier. Once you have done some work on it, try pulling on the ROPE again.

Chapter 6
MORE ON THE ROPE TECHNIQUE

More On Rope

ROPE is a very effective projection technique, but it still has to be learned to be effective. I would like to elaborate on a couple of points about the technique, inspired by the feedback I have received so far.

*1. There is NO visualisation required - AT ALL - in the ROPE technique. It is ALL tactile imaging. This means you do NOT have to picture yourself doing it. That is, to climb ROPE, the correct mental action is to REHEARSE the climbing action in your mind * This mental rehearsal - IS - the ROPE technique ***

*2. You need to *mentally* grit your teeth and strain with the action, i.e., you have to put maximum mental effort into it, as if you were really climbing a ROPE, but without allowing your muscles to take part in it - this is ALL mental. Your body must not be allowed to respond. You also need to feel you are very strong, full of energy and could climb like this all night.*

3. You will find that a certain way of holding the focus of your mind, while you climb, will exert more pressure on your astral body than another. It is VERY important you note what this is and learn how to apply it. This will tune your climbing action for the maximum effect.

When you hit on the right mental focus for the action, you will feel a corresponding dizzy/falling sensation in your Solar Plexus.

4. To use ROPE successfully, it is extremely important to make a firm decision to DO IT. This commitment is VERY important to success. A DO OR DIE effort is needed. This focuses all your mental energy into a single point, for a single purpose - to exit your body.

5. Many people have emailed me with ROPE success stories. In every case - they have been practising ROPE when they suddenly decided to give it a go - TO RE-ALLY DO iT! This commitment to succeed means the difference between actually getting out -OOBE - and experiencing various levels of ROPE induced relaxation, trance, paralysis, chakra activity etc. I cannot stress eno-ugh the importance of this commitment to the success of ROPE induced OOBE.

6. While using ROPE, completely IGNORE ALL physical sensation AND ANY NOISES YOU HEAR. If you react to a sensation, in any way, you will lose the focus of your mental energy and dilute your effort considerably. All the energy/chakra work and other exercises in Parts 3 and 4, are designed to stimulate the flow of energy in your body and increase concentration, will power and mental control. By increasing the energy flow during a projection and controlling your mind better, your duration in real time is increased. It is also easier to exit. You CAN skip all the exercises entirely and just concentrate on learning ROPE. Everyone has different levels of skill, natural ability and energy flow. Some people need lots of training in order to OOBE, others do not. Some people will prefer to learn ROPE by DOiNG it, rather than training for it. If your goal is just to have a conscious OOBE, of any kind, the simple use of ROPE, below, is your best option.

Simple Use Of Rope

Some people have the impression ROPE is too complicated. This was possibly because by the detailed explanation I gave about the mechanics of ROPE in Part 5, i.e., HOW it works.

ROPE is THE simplest projection technique to date. All that is needed to use ROPE in its simplest form, are these two steps:

1. Go to bed, or sit in your chair, relax and settle yourself down, as you normally would do before going to sleep.

2. Start climbing the ROPE.

** This is all there is to the simple use of ROPE **

As there are no time consuming exercises or complicated relaxation exercises involved, the simple use of ROPE has many advantages. It allows you to focus all your mental resources on it. In many cases this is all that is needed to give you your first conscious OOBE.

Because the simple use of ROPE is less complex, you will find yourself attempting projection more often, even when you are tired one of the best times to try - and cannot be bothered with anything complicated. The increased frequency of your projection attempts gives you more practise with ROPE and hence the technique will be mastered sooner.

Lucid Dream Backup

I have had a great many reports of vivid dreams and heightened lucid dream activity (L.D.) from people doing the energy/chakra training exercises. This is happening far too frequently for it to be coincidence.

The energy/chakra work increases the level of energy flowing into the energy body and heightens awareness and memory of the dream and OOBE state. It is a shame to waste all this energy on uncontrolled dreams, so I suggest L.D. be used as a secondary goal. This will give you OOBE experience earlier, in the form of L.D., and help keep your interest high until you learn how to do the conscious exit.

Lucid Dreaming

To become Lucid in dream you need to program yourself with a trigger to make you realise when you are dreaming, in order to take control over it, i.e., become lucid. The best way of doing this is by getting into the habit of doing frequent reality checks during your daily life.

Reality Checking

A reality check is when you stop what you are doing and check the reality level of your situation. This is simple to do. Every time you do a reality check.

Ask yourself:

1. is this a normal situation, is there anything strange about it?

2. Can I fly? Try floating up in the air.

3. Try closing your eyes. This is a dead giveaway as you cannot close your eyes in astral form.

Note: This reality checking must become habitual to be effective.

When you do a reality check during a dream, you will realise you are dreaming and can take control of it. It is then important to affirm to yourself you are going to remember everything. Tell yourself over and over, " I will remember this when I wake up."

L.D. Trigger

The key to success with reality checks is to have a good trigger for it. This should be something you would normally do many times a day. This can be any kind of habitual action, but here are a few ideas:

1. Time: Every time you look at your watch, do a reality check. An electronic watch is a good aid. Set the timer to beep hourly. When it beeps, do a reality check.

* A wrist watch, beeping hourly, is the most effective

2. Hands: Every time you notice your hands, do a reality check.

3. Smoking: if you smoke, every time you have a cigarette, do a reality check. You will usually find yourself reaching for a cigarette during the course of a dream, if you are a habitual smoker.

Note: it takes time to make your trigger habitual, usually a few weeks. It also helps to do a few affirmations before you go to sleep, e.g., "I will remember to look at my watch".

When you become aware in a dream, L.D., you should already be in a communal dream pool. If you want to try changing this to a real time projection, try and become aware of your physical body. If you can sense it, you may be able to return to a time location near it. This is difficult, though, and may end the experience completely, i.e., forcing a return to the waking state. I suggest you enjoy the L.D. for what it is. Communal dream pools are very colourful places and usually lots of fun. You will see all kinds of weird and wonderful things there and have all kinds of adventures.

Note: To improve your memory of the L.D. don't forget to remind yourself constantly during the L.D., to remember it all.

Changing Your Reality Location

If you don't like the dream pool you are in, or are in a real time OOBE and want to enter a dream pool, here are a couple of ways to do it:

1. Look closely at your hands and watch them melt. (This is worth doing just to see the melting hands phenomenon).

2. Spin around until you become disoriented.

3. Visualise a place you would like to be. (instantaneous travel). This will usually move you to a dream pool similar to your visualised target destination.

4. Fly straight up, as fast as you can. If this fails to shift your reality location, at least you will experience space flight.

5. Fly away fast, close to the surface, until you find a place you like. The blurring of speed will cause a reality shift.

6. Walk into a mirror, picture or painting. This is the same as VRP (virtual reality projection).

These techniques all trick the subconscious, through dis-orientation, into moving you to another reality location.

The Astral Form In Motion

Many people have motion problems in their first few projections. Simply getting across a room in the right direction, can be a major accomplishment.

This lack of control is simply because they are unfamiliar with astral form. It is like being in zero gravity. You have to learn to move all over again. When you project in real time, you are just a point of consciousness with a poorly constructed etheric shell surrounding it. Motion is provided by thought - not muscles.

Astral Momentum

There is a type of momentum in astral form that causes most of the problems. This causes you to continue moving for a while, after you decide to stop. This may take you through a wall or a ceiling etc. This impetus is caused by the thought you used to cause the motion. If it is too strong, or too prolonged for the action, you will move too quickly or too far. Only practise teaches you how to get about with any degree of accuracy and grace.

It really is quite a comical process, learning astral motion.

I remember learning to move about my home town, in my youth. I would start by trying to navigate through my house, usually ending up stuck in the roof, for a while. Then I would run down the road, trying to build up speed and take off like a plane. I would get airborne for a while, but could never quite clear the roof tops of the surrounding houses. I would often float unintentionally into strange houses, blundering about like a drunk in zero G.

I seemed to be endlessly apologising to all these strangers in passing, as I floated in and out of their houses.

How To Move

To move about in astral form, simply - DO iT. Do not think about what you are doing, just DO iT. Be aware that motion is provided by your mind. You have to will yourself into motion, to change direction, and to stop. This is the best advice I can give you on this. It really has to be learned by doing. Have fun.

When you have learned basic motion, do not try anything too ambitious for a while. Stick close to the surface and learn to get around your local area first. Practise varying your speed until you gain some control over it.

Learning To Fly

Learn to fly the same way as you learned to move, by using your mind. At first you may find something very much like gravity affecting you. You may get yourself into the air only to find yourself slowly arcing back to earth again. If you persevere you'll find yourself moving in a series of short flight hops. This is caused partly by habit and partly by the basic motion problem in general. You sink back to earth when your motion causing mental action falters. This causes your flight impetus to stop and the gravity habit then pulls you down.

You may find yourself, as I did, trying to fly by running down the road and leaping into the air. This is not necessary. Focus your will into floating up into the air. Then use your will to provide motion, same as with basic motion. There is NO gravity affecting you in astral form. Convince yourself of this and you will be flying in no time.

Speed

The three speeds as defined by, S. Muldoon, and commonly accepted, are a basic guide only. These are:

1. Walking speed.

2. Motor car speed.

3. Instantaneous travel.

I think these three speeds were a sign of the times back then. These would have been the only types of speed known to most people. Today, movies, computer games and air travel have thoroughly prepared our minds to accept much higher speeds.

With practise and good mental control, you CAN vary your speed to your purpose, from walking speed to supersonic speed. This is a big problem for the beginner though, the control of direction and speed. It has a lot to do with how stable the projection is and how experienced you are at applying your will to motion.

Instantaneous Travel

It is generally accepted that if you can visualise a destination you can project yourself there instantly, at the speed of thought.

* I have found this to be highly unreliable *

I find this instantaneous method usually projects you

straight into a subjective location created by the visualisation of your target. You may appear to be at your destination but you will usually find many discrepancies between the real location and where you are.

Instantaneous travel is very like VRP. By using your visualisation powers to travel with, you will not actually travel. You will create a subjective copy of a destination and enter it.

Long Distance Travel

I have found it more reliable to follow the surface for short to medium distance projection of up to a few hundred miles. Even this can be difficult as it is easy to fall into the Alice effect while travelling. All you have to do is break concentration once and you will slip into a dream pool. Strict mental control must be maintained at all times when travelling in real time.

It is not really practical to follow the surface for a long distance. For example, a country on the other side of the world from you is 12000 miles away. You would need to travel at about 64 times the speed of sound to reach there in 15 minutes. At this speed in the atmosphere, everything blurs and clouds and surface features cause disorientation and a corresponding reality shift. Any real time objective aspect of the projection will then be lost. Note: Newbie projectors can normally hold themselves in real time for only a few minutes. Therefore, any long distance travel is limited by the real time part of a projection.

To travel long distance you need to study geography. You have to be able to recognise continents, oceans, countries, states and cities. You also need to study a map of your target area and note any landmarks. To project there, after this is memorised, you must go into orbit and re-enter over your target. As you approach the earth you must adjust your approach and aim for the geological features and landmarks around your destination.

Orbiting the Earth

To enter orbit is a little more difficult than it sounds. Getting up there is easy, you just go straight up, but stopping when you get high enough is difficult. Most people, myself included, tend to blast themselves straight out of the solar system, sometimes right out of the galaxy. To avoid this, it is important to control your speed during the ascent.

It is easier to project to the moon first, as a way of entering orbit. This gives you a large visual target you can project to in moments. Once there, it is a simple matter to head back to Earth, enter orbit, and circle until you are above your target. In space, away from the atmosphere, there are no problems with speed induced blurring.

How Far Can You Go?

*There are * NO * limits to distance, destination or speed. You can travel to the most distant galaxy. The speed of thought is infinite. It is like folding space and moving without moving. If you can see something, you can be there....as quick as that. In comparison, the speed of light is that of a snail. I often go out into deep space, where the galaxies are just tiny smudges in the distance, to think and meditate. That is easy, but the trick is getting back for a conscious re-entry. Unless you have a good knowledge of astronomy, which I do not, this is difficult. Following the silver cord, if you can see one, is not practical at that kind of speed, though it will give you a basic direction to go in.*

To return from a long distance projection, tune into your body and become aware of it. Then try moving part of your physical body, i.e., a finger or toe.

This will return you to your body, and end the projection with full memories of the OOBE.

Future Wind

There is a strange phenomenon you will come across, from time to time, while you are projecting. I call this

"Future Wind."

You will be OOBE'ing somewhere, minding your own business, when all of a sudden you will feel an irresistible force. You will feel yourself being moved against your will, usually backwards, by this force. You can fight it for a while but it will grow steadily stronger until you are blown away; over the roof tops, up into the sky and.... into the future.

Then, after a while, you will come down in a different place....and time.

Often it will be somewhere mundane, maybe a domestic setting of some sort. You will be released there and left to wander about... confused. You may even meet people you do not know, yet, and they will be just as confused as you are.

This may be an actual scene out of your future life, it may be a symbolic vision, or a mixture of both. You may be an invisible spectator to this scene, or you may merge with your future self, and see out of your future eyes for while.

This can also be a scene of an important future event. It could be a disaster, natural or otherwise, or something unusual or exciting on the world scene.

These type of events usually have a lot of energy surrounding them, and this may be part of the reason for the vision.

The only explanations I can give for this are:

1. The intervention of your higher self: For some reason it decides that now is the time to show you something from your future.
2. Clairvoyant interference: Your Brow chakra has become clairvoyantly active and has tuned into a future setting. Your point of consciousness is caught up by this vision and projected into the vision.

3. A combination of both of the above - this is the most logical.

Symbolic Visions

There is another aspect of this wind that is very similar to the above but the vision you experience is symbolic, or has a symbolic aspect, rather than an actual future event or scene.

Note: I would like to warn you about the symbolic aspect of visions. If you don't understand the nature of symbolism it can cause great harm to your life. This warning applies to all clairvoyant visions in general, whether experienced in astral form or not.

For example: You are taken, by a future wind, to a scene in which you see yourself winning a lot of money. You are sitting at a table checking your lottery ticket with the results. You see the prize money is $18 million. You check your numbers, or ticket, and find you have the winning ticket. You feel all the excitement, the surge of adrenalin, dreams of wealth come flooding into you and your heart races with excitement.

After this vision, you start buying lots of tickets. You also start to make decisions that affect your life with a "When the money comes through" type of attitude. This can cause irreparable damage to your life! You lose your drive, your initiative, your ambition, i.e., you stop trying. This imparts a "Cargo Cult" type of belief system on you, a belief that everything will be given to you - with all the negative aspects this primitive belief system has. This can cause you to mark time in your life, instead of living it to the full.

** What you may have missed, from the symbolism of the above vision is:*

The amount of money may be unusual for that lottery draw. $18 million is an odd amount of money and may be a rare event. This is what I call a SIGN POST - a date stamp of a future event. This means that when your local lottery has a prize of the above amount, something important is going to happen in your life or in the world around you. If you know how symbolism works, during the vision you would have been able to pick up more information about this coming event. The setting, the symbols, the connections to you, the action and the *sequence of events in it, are all important aspects of its meaning. Misunderstanding a vision can ruin your life. Only experience and the intelligent application of logic can teach you how to interpret a symbolic vision. Until you have this experience, it is best to treat any sort of vision with caution.*

Some possible reasons for a symbolic vision are:

1. You are being given a warning or guidance by your higher self.

2. You are being given proof there is a future, a destiny, a meaning, a purpose to your life.

3. The sign post of this vision may mark a good or bad event in your life.

4. You may actually win the lottery. Personally, I would always make sure I had a ticket in the draw, just in case, but I would not depend on it.

Future Wind Example

I left my body and was moving about my home, getting my sea legs.

Suddenly, a force moved me across the room. I tried to fight it but it grew stronger until I was blown out of the house and up into the night sky. A short time later I was brought down again, outside my home. I was just left standing there in the middle of the road. In front of me stood a refrigerator.

It was just sitting there in the road with its door open. I examined it and could tell it was not working. Behind it was a massive red brick wall, 40 feet high and twice as wide. There are no REAL brick walls in this street. Then I noticed my wife was standing beside me. I turned and said hello to her.

She just said goodbye, very coldly, then turned and walked away. Perplexed, I watched her walk away. Oddly, instead of walking to our home, she walked away from it and off into the distance.

Being experienced with the symbolism and nature of visions I knew what this foretold, the end of my marriage. I could not understand it as we were only recently married and very happy together.

To decipher a symbolic vision it is necessary to analyse it and break it down into its parts.

The six significant aspects of this vision are:

*1. The sign post... (the date stamp of the event) * The refrigerator that did not work.*

*The connections... (something, or someone, in the vision that connects the events to me). ***

1. My wife.

2. It was outside my home.

3. I was there as me.

2. The symbol... (the basic nature of the coming event)

** The large brick wall. This symbolises a barrier or an end to something. This was the only actual symbol in the vision, but other parts of it were by nature or action - symbolic.*

3. The symbolic action... (this signifies the meaning of the vision) * My wife's cold goodbye.

4. The symbolic modifiers... (these modify the symbol or, in this case, the symbolic action in the vision). a) My wife departed in a direction away from our home. b) She walked away until she disappeared from view.

5. The sequence of events:
1. The broken fridge.
2. The large brick wall.
3. My wife's actions.

OR: When I saw the broken fridge (sign post) I saw the brick wall (symbol) and my wife (connection) said goodbye and left (symbolic action) in a direction away from our home, until she disappeared (symbolic modifiers) The timing and sequence of a vision is important to unravelling its meaning.

It is important to break a symbolic vision into its 5 basic parts and to note this in your journal, while it is still fresh in your mind.

Note: There may be more than one modifier to each part of a vision.

Hindsight

A year after I had the above vision, we moved to another town. The day we moved, we had to borrow a refrigerator from a relative. Ours had broken down and was in for repairs. The borrowed fridge did not work either. After ours was repaired, this other fridge sat on our porch for two and a half years, waiting to be collected. I remembered the vision clearly, and knew this fridge was the date stamp of an upcoming event. I also knew what the event was, but honestly could not see it happening. One day, though, they came and collected this fridge. A week later my marriage ended. Suddenly, permanently, and for no foreseeable reason.

Looking at it in hind sight, it is crystal clear what the vision meant. It was as simple as it was accurate. Most symbolic visions are this simple. Be very careful not to read too much into vision otherwise the true message in the vision will be obscured.

Always break a vision down into its parts.

Ask of each part:

1. *"What is it in itself?"*
2. *"What does it do?"*
3. *"What is its simplest, most basic, symbolic meaning?"*

Write these

answers down and then apply common sense and logic to them. This will give you insight into the true meaning of the vision.

Mirrors

Mirrors, historically, are magical devices used as doorways to other worlds.

There are also numerous superstitions and old wives tales concerning their effect on the recently departed. After a person had died, all mirrors in their home were covered. This was so they could not see their lack of a reflection and be shocked. Another reason for this was to prevent them from being accidentally trapped in a mirror.

There is some logic to this if you look at the mechanics of projection. Death, in the early stages, is very much like a powerful real time projection. The biggest difference being the lack of a living body to return to.

Spirits are normally held close to the physical dimension, in real time, for a week or so after death. This is until the supply of etheric matter that binds the spirit to its physical body runs out.

During this time it is normal for the spirit to wander among relatives and loved ones, saying goodbye and coming to terms with their new state of existence. This goodbye process, eases the psychological trauma of death, and helps prepare the spirit for the next stage of existence.

What can happen with mirrors, is this: A new spirit can inadvertently enter a mirror. If this happens, they enter a mirror world in the same way a projector enters a picture through VRP. Once in a mirror world they usually do not know where they are, or how to get out of it, and can be stuck there for the duration of their real time stay. This will not interfere with the journey of the soul. It will just cause confusion for a few days until it enters the next stage of existence. This can though, make their last days near the physical world very confusing and interfere in the natural goodbye process.

This, I believe, is where the old superstitions came from. Therefore, in the light of my understanding of projection and the death process, I think the covering of mirrors after a death is a VERY good idea, for the benefit of the deceased. This is best done for two weeks, to be sure.

A Better Goodbye

It is possible to communicate with a recently departed spirit during its real time, post death wandering. This can be done by leaving a letter, uncovered, for the spirit to read. They can also hear you, so talking to them is also effective. I think a good practise would be to have goodbye letters, from all the people that loved the deceased, stuck to the wall in the spirit's old room. Leave the letters open, with all pages clearly in view, to make reading easier.

Chapter 7
OOBE AND DUALITY

OOBE & Duality:

If you read the enormous number of case histories available on out of body and near death experiences; you will find many accounts hinting at perceptions of duality which indicate symptoms of the mind split effect at work. It is fairly common, during an OOBE, to be aware of the physical body while also being aware of existing in the projected double, or less commonly, vice-versa. This effect appears to indicate the existence of telepathic and bio-energetic links between the physical body and it's remote projected double (possibly via the silver cord). This link appears to serve the purpose of providing the projected double with the necessary energies it requires whilst operating out of body, while also maintaining an unbreakable connection with its physical body. This connection also allows the physical body to be, in many ways, monitored (or sensed) so that no harm can come to it during an OOBE.

During an OOBE, at the moment the projected double is generated and projected from the physical body, the projector's mind effectively splits into two identical parts (mirror images) each containing a complete copy of thinking mind and memory. One copy always remains firmly locked inside the physical body (original hard copy) while a mirror image is reflected into and maintained in the exterior projected double.

The splitting of consciousness into two (or more) separate but identical copies happens during sleep or any kind of OOBE. I call this effect "The Mind Split Effect":

Mental/Visual Feedback:

If a mentally awake physical mind happens to observe (with real time or astral sight) it's projected double at close range during a projection, a strong visual and telepathic connection can form between them. This can be a very disturbing experience and I don't recommend this be tried for more than a few seconds at a time. The awake physical mind (whilst a projection is in progress) must see and be seen by its projected double for this type of connection to occur. Vision, seeing each other at the same time, appears necessary for this type of connection to occur. Once this happens, each side of the mind split, physical and projected, connect and begin to see out of each other's eyes at the same time. Each becomes aware of each other's vision and perspective as well as that of their own.

Once the visual side of this connection occurs, each side of the mind split instantly becomes aware of each other's thought's as well, simultaneously and compounding. This appears to be something like telepathic feedback, much like holding two identical 'mental' mirrors facing each other. This gives an unnatural glimpse of mental infinity - a mental reflection of a mental reflection of a mental reflection, continually compounding.

When two identical minds connect, while separated during an oobe, the two identical sets of vision and thoughts create something that can best be described as a visual and telepathic loop, compounding and feeding back upon itself in a never ending loop. This is an unnatural, incomprehensible, disturbing and possibly dangerous event for any mortal mind to experience. This uncomfortable and confusing state appears to only occur at close range and can easily be avoided by not looking too closely at each other (physical and projected double) and by not thinking at each other at close range (within approximately twenty feet) during a real time projection.

Note: this can only happen if both sides of a projector, physical and projected, are awake and become visually aware of each other during a real time projection. This all goes a long way towards explaining why dreams and projection memories can sometimes appear so chaotic. The mind splits for a very good reason and the separated copies are meant to function separately.

I have experimented with this phenomena many times during real time projections, after discovering it accidentally during a powerful real time OOBE. I recreated the original 'accident' and studied it because the original experience raised so many questions. I had always been curious of the way I could often feel my physical body while close to it, and this mind split effect appeared to hold many of the answers I had been searching for.

Like many other projectors, I had often experienced confusing anomalies during projections: of being aware of events and noises near my physical body, in and around my house, plus being aware of my remote existence during a projection. This sense of perceived duality, of having two different sets of perception, one physical and one remote, has been reported by many other projectors but has never, I believe, been properly studied or understood.

Double Trouble:

Here is an account of one of the first times I experienced the mind split effect and mental/visual feedback: I had been meditating in my chair by the fire and returned to normal awareness as the rain started drumming on the roof. The weather was pretty wild and the wind was starting to shake the windows and doors. I looked at the clock, it was almost 3 AM. This was not unusual for me, as sometimes I will meditate all night. I felt well rested and full of energy and thought to myself "I've never projected in a storm before, I wonder what it's like?" Closing my eyes once again, I relaxed back into myself and soon projected out of my body, using the 'point shift' method, as given in Vol 1 of the Treatise. This method is very similar to the method given by T.Lobsang Rampa in his book 'You Forever'. While this method is more difficult than the Rope method, given in Vol 2, it is very effective and is the original method I learned when I first taught myself conscious exit projection. I have been projecting since the age of 4 or 5, but this was always spontaneous and I had little control of when I would project. I taught myself to project deliberately at the age of 21, and found Rampa's books a great help?

As a side note: many people have claimed that Lobsang Rampa was discredited, that he was 'exposed' as being nothing more than an English plumber cum writer on metaphysics. But, if you read his first book 'The Third Eye' you'll see that he fully explained his circumstances, and how he came to be living in the body of an English Plumber. He claims to have swapped bodies with a suicidal English plumber who was about to kill himself -while his own Tibetan body lay dying of wounds. This feat was accomplished during an astral operation carried out by high ranking Tibetan masters (spirit masters) to preserve Rampa's unfinished life path, while freeing the

Plumber (with his full permission) who was at the exact end of his life.

Personally, I found Rampa's books to be very good reading, and they contain a great deal of useful information on projection, clairvoyance, metaphysics, etc.) Back to the projection: After exiting my body I moved through the wall and floated out into the rain drenched night. What a gloriously wet feeling that was. I could feel and taste the cool rain and blustering wind passing through me. The smell of rain and wetness was everywhere, seeming to fill me with a bright and happy energy. I floated up to the roof and sat on the chimney, looking out over the town. I felt a little bit like a very wet Mary Poppins. I watched the rain dancing over the roofs and streets, swirling through gutters and gurgling into drains. It seemed to have a friendly voice and rhythm all its own "drink me, splash me, gurgle me, slosh me." (It seemed funny at the time:)

While sitting on the roof, I felt my body stirring in room chair below me. This effect had often intrigued me and I decided to slide back through the roof and study it more closely.

As I passed through the roof I saw my body sitting in the chair, right where I had left it, but suddenly I became aware of also watching my projected double (from my perspective in the chair) sliding down through the ceiling both at the same time! It was ME, sitting in the chair watching another ME floating down through the ceiling, but it was also ME floating in front of my chair some ten feet away - watching myself sitting in the chair. This was not only confusing, it started making me feel quite ill. I had two sets of vision and two sets of thoughts, all at the same time and all joined together, it was fascinating. It also made a lot of sense. Just because the projected ME was outside its physical body, why should the physical ME have to stop thinking. Why would it be left (as is commonly believed today) as a mere empty shell during a projection? This raises the question of 'what' actually leaves the physical body during a projection?

The projected ME (real time double) moved about the room, observing my physical body in the chair - while it watched me back at the same time. I could still see the projected ME, even when my projected double was situated behind the physical ME. I could feel myself in the chair perfectly, as I tried to follow the movements of my projected double about the room. This took some very real effort, and it also took a lot of energy to move my projected double. It felt like I was moving through thick mud and I felt an enormous pressure building up inside both of ME.

I was existing in both my physical body as well as in my projected double - both at the 'same' time. I was fully awake (mentally) and aware and thinking inside both aspects of myself. Inside my physical body, my conscious-ness appeared to be actively centred in my etheric body, and this appeared to be how the physical ME was able to see the projected ME (real time sight - seeing through closed eyelids). I came to this conclusion because of the way I could move around 'inside' my physical body, and could even see behind myself without physically moving. My etheric body appeared to be, quite literally, able to turn around inside my physical body.

This ability of the physical body to see through closed eyelids and from different perspectives is frequently described by projectors and trance meditators.

Note: The etheric body appears to be the very first level of subtle body, one stage up from the physical body. This appears to be so closely enmeshed within the physical body that it cannot normally leave its confines while it still lives. During the full trance state, as well as during the projection process, however, it appears to gain some limited freedom of movement. It will also often gain the ability to see into the real time zone, and sometimes even into the astral dimension, around it. The etheric body appears to be responsible for the ability to see through closed eyelids and covers, as is often reported by projectors near the exit stage of a projection.

My observations: the centre of waking consciousness appears to shift over 'into' the etheric body when the physical body enters the trance state and falls asleep. This is very like an internal projection, taking a 'reflection' of consciousness one step away from the physical body and mind, while still holding its original place within the confines of the physical body. This stage, I believe, is the very first level of the multi dimensional projection process, and is marked by the 'heaviness' experienced when the full trance state is entered, which is also the sign the physical body has fallen asleep.

This process makes a lot of sense and answers a lot of questions when projection case histories, plus the 'mechanics' and 'dynamics' of projection, are studied. It points to projection being a staggered process where consciousness is reflected one stage at a time away from the physical body and mind. Each stage becomes progressively more subtle and refined, while still maintaining firm telepathic and energetic links between each stage.

Basically, this allows the projection of all the higher subtle bodies at the same time, while keeping a safe and unbreakable link between them and the physical body (the original hard copy).

Projection Stages:

The list below shows the physical body as (0) with the dream mind marked as (-1) below it, and the first four stages of higher subtle bodies above it.

4 = Mental body, and above.

3 = Astral body.

2 = Real time body.

1 = Etheric body.

0 = Physical body. (base line)

-1 = Dream mind

The Incredible Mind Split:

A projector's mind splits during any kind of OOBE. One complete copy (original hard physical copy) staying at all times safely inside the physical body, capable of thinking and dreaming. A perfect thinking copy, containing full memories, both conscious and subconscious, 'reflects' into the extruded real time body. Each copy is capable of thinking and acting independently during an oobe if enough vital energy (vitality) is available. Neither copy may be aware of the other's continuing existence or awake state. This is the natural mind-split effect which always occurs, but is very seldom noticed, during sleep and all types of OOBE. During a conscious exit projection, consciousness is first reflected into the etheric body. From the etheric body it is then reflected into the real time 'projectable' double when that body is generated. The real time double appears to be generated inside the combined physical/etheric bodies and does not appear to project outside the physical/etheric body until a copy of consciousness is transferred (reflected) into it. Before the actual moment of projection, of the exit of the real time body out of the physical body, all potential copies of mind are closely enmeshed and held together safely inside the physical body. One full copy always stays inside the physical/etheric body and this (the original copy) appears to fall asleep and thus moves itself safely, but temporarily, out of the picture to allow the natural projection process to occur. The original copy of mind will begin dreaming at some point after it falls asleep. If the original copy does not move itself out of the picture, the difficulty of projection increases dramatically, as with conscious exit projection where the mind is awake throughout the projection process. This last factor alone accounts for the sheer difficulty of conscious exit projection.

The dreaming mind of the physical body appears to account for the reality fluctuations commonly experienced shortly after the exit stage of a projection. This event may also be associated with the physical body's dream mind entering the REM sleep state (REM = Rapid Eye Movement) which is commonly associated with the dreaming state. The physical body's dreaming mind also appears to account for the hypnagogic imagery and visions experienced during the trance state and during the pre-projection state, or where the mind is held awake and balancing on the verge of sleep.

At the moment of separation, as the real time body projects free of the physical/etheric bodies, the mind appears to split or reflect a complete copy of itself into an 'exterior' subtle body. From this moment onwards both copies, one internal and one external, continuing to record their memories separately. Neither will usually be aware of the other's presence or existence, apart from the occasional vaguely shared feelings and remote percep-tions of each other. The separateness of the mind-split effect and memory recording will continue until reinte-gration occurs. Upon reintegration, or waking, only one set of memories will usually be retained, but sometimes a mixture will occur. This can be part dream, part physi-cal/etheric and part OOBE memories. The successful 'downloading' of projection memories strong enough to override physical/etheric body and dream memories for the same time period, strong enough to leave a lasting impression on the physical brain of a projector, appears to be the real key to successful and repeatable OOBE. See my new book "ASTRAL DYNAMICS" Chapter 21 - Overcoming The Mind Split -for more detailed informa-tion on this.

Mind Split Effects:

It is fairly common for projector's to experience a perfect projection right up until the exit, where they fee l all the vibrations, rapid heartbeat, floating sensation, etc., and then it all just 'goes away'. This leaves the projector, usually energetically exhausted, often partially or fully paralysed, thinking they have simply failed the exit. What may often happen in cases like this are normal and successful OOBE's, but where consciousness has remained awake and 'centred' in the 'physical/etheric' mind after the mind split of projection has occurred. The resulting memories retained after the experience, in cases like this, are thus from the physical/etheric side of the experience only.

The projected double, in many cases, simply stays out of its body for too long, which allows the physical/etheric mind's to fall into a deep sleep. Once deep sleep occurs, the projected double becomes effectively locked out of its physical/etheric body for the duration of sleep, or until waking occurs. (re why I recommend short projections) The projection side of this experience (the memory of it) has thus been totally lost, as if it never was. The physical/etheric mind (internal) side of the experience has the only solid memories for the whole experience, and the projected double's memories have failed to make a strong enough impression on the physical brain to become 'memorable' after reintegration. Basically, the projection memories have failed to make the final 'wrinkle' in the physical brain after the projection.

Another mind-split also appears to occur between the real time double and the astral body. This begins to happen 'naturally' within several minutes of the start of an average real time projection, but can often occur within a few seconds. At some point during any real time projection reality will always begin to fluctuate. This appears to be the sign that the physical/etheric mind has begun dreaming. At this point the real time body usually begins to run low on energy (in most cases, apparently not having enough energy to maintain its conscious integrity whilst the dream mind is active) and it thus starts shifting into the seemingly more easily maintained (but more dimensionally remote) astral vehicle in the astral dimension. Soon, the real time body will effectively fall asleep and will then be reeled in to hover, as if asleep, just above the sleeping physical body. It will remain there until the natural waking of the physical body and mind causes reintegration of all its multi-dimensional aspects, thus ending the mind split.

Notes On Projection & Reintegration:

1. The sleep state, or trance state, is required for projection to occur.

2. Trance = body asleep + mind awake.

3. The waking state is required for reintegration to occur.

4. The only exception to the above is the in-between trance state, where the body is asleep but the mind is fully awake.

5. Deep sleep prohibits reintegration of physical/etheric and projected doubles.

I know this may all sound a little complex, but it sheds a great deal of light on many of the seemingly mysterious difficulties which can beset a projector. It also explains why projections are so time limited and difficult to maintain, let alone remember in detail. All through my research and studies, in the incredibly complex field of theoretical metaphysics, I have found that the further I get from the relatively normal reality of the physical dimension the more outrageously complicated everything becomes. There is nothing simple about the mechanics and dynamics of projection, far from it, but it can be understood if the lower levels of projection are studied, i.e., etheric and real time bodies. If the principals this yields are then applied to the higher aspects of projection, and even dreaming, a few precious constant factors appear. This methodology may not solve all problems, nor answer all questions, but it at least provides some kind of a logical and understandable framework to work in.

Purpose Of Mind Split:

The mind split is, I believe, an integral part of the workings of Universal Law, where the mind splits and reflects itself into many different parts, levels and aspects, each belonging to a different dimensional level.

During the full multi-mind-split process, the highest level (highest subtle body) appears to be drawn into the centre of the universe, into the Source of all conscious-

ness, by what I have called the Akashic Pulse. There,
the influential and conditional energies (consciousness
seeds), contained within each individual energy egg
(each person) are processed and updated according
to Universal Law. These are adjusted according to past
and current thoughts and actions, and as further modi-
fied by Karmic Law.

These seeds affect and influence us all profoundly.
They cause the attraction and repulsion effect, all our
likes and dislikes and natural tendencies, which are
the visible workings of Universal Law in the physical
dimension.

Universal Law is that which attempts to guide us all
along our individual life's paths, towards predetermined
but eminently variable goals (variable according to laws
of free will and individual choices).

An important aspect of the mind split, to many people,
is the way it shows how the physical body and its mind
are 'never' 'ever' left empty and unguarded during sleep
or any type of out of body experience or projection.

They are thus never exposed to being entered, molested, possessed or interfered with by any other projector, or by any type of inorganic being, entity or demon. A conscious exit projector's physical body and mind are, according to my research, fir more projected than they are during the full waking state - where natural nonphysical senses become somewhat dulled or inactive. During an OOBE, the projector's energy body appears to expand and create a very sensitive perimeter, a kind of expanded energy cocoon around itself. This appears to extend in all directions for approximately 20 feet (6 metres) often filling or overflowing from the room around the projector's physical body. This sensitive energy perimeter acts something like an early warning system. If it is broached by another 'awake' person, another projector, or any other type of energy being or entity, and a negative reaction occurs, it will instantly snap shut and reel back the projector for immediate reintegration and the return of full waking consciousness. This early warning system appears to be particularly sensitive during any type of conscious OOBE, where the projected double is fully aware it is out of its body. It seems, however, to become slightly less sensitive to 'real' awake people once the physical body and mind have fallen into a deep sleep. It will, however, always react violently and instantly if touched by-anything which causes a negative reaction in its perimeter field.

ULTRA Short OOBE:

One of the most important things to do after a successful exit, especially the first few times, is to keep the projection ultra short. Ten seconds out and then get straight back into the physical body. Please trust me on this. Ten seconds of REAL out of body experience with a fully conscious exit and reentry, are worth a thousand all nighters that are forgotten! An ultra short oobe is, in most cases, the 'major' contributing factor to a successful first time conscious exit projection.

Once again, if a projector stays out too long, especially a novice projector, and their physical/etheric body falls into a deep sleep, the projected double will not usually be able to reanimate its physical body and mind when it returns. It can thus become locked out for the duration of the projection, or until natural waking occurs. Projection requires the physical body to fall asleep, and the reverse applies, with reintegration requiring the physical body to wake up. If the physical body and mind fall into a deep sleep, sometimes even a good shaking will fail to wake them. The slight energy rush caused by re-entry can thus also fail to awaken a deeply sleeping, and possibly dreaming, physical body and mind.

Projected Double Contact:

One way of cementing projection memories is to make contact with yourself during an OOBE. Keeping in mind the nature of the mind split, agree with yourself to try and make contact from both sides of the projection, from both physical and projected sides. Some degree of real time sight (seeing through closed eyelids in physical body) is required for this. Agree for your projected double to be in a particular place, say the foot of the bed, and that it will look and think at where your physical head is, or should be. Do this even if the physical or projected double cannot clearly see its counterpart - which often happens on both sides. Often only a vague ghostly shape is seen, or a depression in the bed. The physical body should trust its projected double will be doing this and should try to do the same, by thinking and concentrating and 'feeling' for where it's projected double is 'supposed' to be. Once contact is made, memories will flood both ways and will become cemen-

ted - making a strong and lasting impression upon the physical brain.

After the initial contact, the projected double should move away quickly to avoid nauseating mental/visual feedback problems. This connection and memory downloading process, if successful, can allow the duration of real time projections to be dramatically extended. The projected double can periodically return to its physical counterpart and download (top up) it's projection memories. If this is done, I suggest no more than a few minutes interval between each memory download. The projected double should also re-enter its physical body the moment it detects signs it is tiring, or the moment it begins experiencing reality fluctuations -which is a sure sign the dream mind is becoming active, which indicates the physical mind is falling asleep.

Energy Raising During OOBE:
To increase out of body vitality and capability it is important to have enough energy flowing from the physical/etheric bodies to the projected double.

This is best done by the projected double while it is out

of body. It must reach out and 'feel' itself sucking energy into itself, feeling energy rushing into it from its physical body. This out of body awareness action appears to create a strong energy demand in the projected double, which causes an increased flow of energy from the physical/etheric body to meet this demand. The increase in the clarity and ability this can cause during a projection can be quite amazing, and happens very quickly. This technique is especially useful if you have projection vision problems or blindness.

Everything will noticeably brighten and light will be seen all around the projector, lighting up the darkness and following them about wherever you go. This technique can be used with great effect to solve or ease most common projected double related weakness problems, visual or otherwise.

Improved Relaxation Technique

Note: This new set of 'improved' and 'simplified' deep physical relaxation exercises are to replace those in the original Treatise.

The first big hurdle you need to overcome is deep phy-

*sical relaxation. With the thousands of letters I have
had from people having problems achieving OOBE
- one problem area stands way out, DEEP PHYSICAL
RELAXATION.*

*Everyone seems to rush through learning this, most
important of skills, to get on with the more interesting
stuff, like the projection attempt itself. But, as with any
type of metaphysical development (metaphysical = mind
science) any skill not thoroughly learned will eventually
stop the aspirant cold, forcing them right back to the
beginning to learn it properly before they can proceed.
More time must be spent learning the skill of totally
relaxing your physical body than with any other skill - it
is THAT important. Relaxation is a progressive skill that
can be learned and improved with time and practise.
The biggest problem with deep physical relaxation, in
the early stages, is that it takes so long that if done properly as part of a projection attempt the projector can
become mentally exhausted or bored. This can ruin a
projection attempt as the projector may then have little
energy or enthusiasm for the exit. if this becomes a
problem, I suggest deep physical relaxation be learned
and practised regularly but 'separately' from projection*

attempts, until such time as the projector can attain deep physical relaxation fairly quickly.

A deep level of physical relaxation is absolutely necessary to consciously project your astral body. This is quite easy to achieve, though, if you go about it in the right way and practice regularly.

Deep physical relaxation plus a clear mind = Trance State The trance state is achieved when the physical body goes to sleep while the mind stays awake and in control of itself. A conscious exit projector needs to be able to attain some level of the trance state before they can successfully project out of their body. Deep physical relaxation leads to and naturally brings about the trance state. The trance state is entered automatically once the physical body enters a deeply enough relaxed state. "Important Note: Just as sleep is possible without deep physical relaxation, so is the trance state. It is quite easy to fall asleep and even enter the trance state while stressed and full of tension, relying on physical/mental tiredness to overcome lack of relaxation and trance ability. Just because you feel the sensations of trance (i.e., heavy body feeling) it does not mean you have attained deep physical relaxation. Many people do this and think they have found a handy short cut, only to find conscious exit projection virtually impossible. Most people, in this case, will fail right on the exit, because their physical body is too tense.

The above is also why sleeping for a few hours first, then waking for a projection attempt, works better for most people who lack relaxation and trance ability. The body has time (sleep) to overcome its sleep deficit and physical tension. This makes projection much easier and is a good way to get early results with conscious exit projection.

Physical relaxation:

Seating:

I suggest sitting in a comfortable arm chair, with good arm and neck support, and a pillow under your feet. The pillow is necessary because when relaxed to a deep level, supporting muscles in the feet will tend to relax and can cause some discomfort.

If an arm chair is not available, use a high backed dining chair. It is possible to use a bed, but falling asleep can be a big problem. If a bed must be used, I suggest laying on the back (never the side) with hands and forearms held vertically above the bed, with elbows resting comfortably on the bed. Adjust and vary this position slightly for comfort. This position will reduce the likelihood of falling asleep.

Dress:

Wear loose, comfortable clothing and bare feet (or loose socks) depending on the local temperature. Tight clothing and shoes will cause discomfort with deep relaxation, and will also restrict the flow of blood and energy.

Posture:

Good posture helps a great deal with deep relaxation. Do not slump in the chair. If good posture is used the body will be well balanced. Then, when a deep level of relaxation is achieved, the body will stay well balanced and will experience no distracting discomfort.

If posture is not good when relaxing deeply, muscles will relax and the body will sag, causing discomfort in the spine and joints, which will interfere with the level of *relaxation attained. Put a pillow behind the lower back and one behind the neck, if necessary, to make sure the body is not sagging.*

Tensing and relaxing muscle groups:
I have kept the relaxation exercises as simple as possible. All that is required is to progressively tense and relax opposing groups of muscles. If you already know a full body relaxation discipline, stick with it or adapt it to this one, making sure all muscle groups are covered.

• Full body stretch: Stretch your arms and legs, really stretch, as if you were very tired, and take several long, slow, deep breaths.
• Feet and calves: Lift up your toes and tense both feet and both calves at the same time - and then relax them. Curl up your toes and repeat.
• Knees and Thighs: Tense both your thighs, knees and calves at the same time - then relax them. Press down with your heels and tense thighs, calves and feet, then relax them.
• Hips, buttocks and groin: Push your buttocks backwards, tense and relax. Push hips forward, tense and relax.

• *Stomach and lower back: Push out your stomach and tense up all stomach muscles, tense and relax. Suck in your stomach and tense lower back and buttocks, tense and relax.*

• *Chest and upper back: Arch shoulders and suck in chest and tense all upper back muscles, tense and relax. Push shoulders back and push out chest and tense all muscles, tense and relax.*

• *Arms: Tense your shoulders, arms and hands, making fists. Pump your arms, bringing fists to shoulders a few times, tense and relax.*

• *Neck: Arch neck forward and place chin on chest and tense all muscles, tense and relax. Push head way back and push chin up high, tense throat and jaw muscles, tense and relax.*

• *Jaw, face and head: Move head back, open mouth wide and screw up face, tensing all muscles in your head, tense and relax. Smile widely while screwing up face, tensing all facial muscles, tense and relax. Frown deeply while screwing up face, tense all facial muscles, tense and relax.*

• *Full body stretch: Give yourself a full body stretch, trying to arch and tense as much of your body as you can, tense and relax.*

*• Repeat the above process until you feel you have relax-
ed your body as much as possible. Each time you do this,
pay particular attention to the relaxation part - letting
your muscles droop and totally relax after tensing
them.*

*• This will get progressively easier to do the more often
you do it. In time, you will be able to relax your entire
body simply by waving your awareness, your mental
hands, over it.*

•MBA Massage:

*• The head and neck areas are the most difficult of all
body parts to relax, as inner tension affects them greatly.
Use awareness actions to massage them. 'Feel' your
'awareness hands' deeply massaging your neck and head,
as if someone were actually massaging them. Use your
memory to recreate the required awareness actions. Feel
your 'hands' penetrating deep within the muscles and
tendons in your head and neck and 'feel' all the tension
leaving your body.*

*• Move your awareness throughout your body, searching
for any tense areas. If you find any, massage them away
until your body is totally relaxed.*

Chapter 8

WAKING PARALYSIS

Waking Paralysis:

Some degree of physical paralysis is a sure sign an OOBE is in PROGRESS. It shows the mind split, in some form, has already occurred. The physical body has varying degrees of difficulty animating itself when the mind split effect is active. Even though they may not be aware a projection is in progress, a projector's physical/etheric body may feel total physical paralysis, or some degree of lethargy and heaviness and disorientation in their physical body.

The degree of this depends greatly upon the strength of the projection and how much energy is being used to maintain it. Strong sensations like these point to an OOBE being in progress.

The degree of paralysis shows the 'strength' of the projection. A full powered Real Time OOBE will cause total physical paralysis (full waking paralysis) while a lighter level of projection can still allow the projector's physical body to stumble to the bathroom - albeit mumbling incoherently and feeling like they are walking on pillows, body fairly numb and fuzzy - but ambulatory all the same.

Waking paralysis (often called sleep paralysis) will also occur where the real time body has been generated 'inside' the physical/etheric body, but actual separation or full projection from the physical/etheric bodies has not occurred. This means a partial projection has occurred, albeit internally, and is causing some degree of waking paralysis. The real time 'projectable double' in this case has not projected completely free of its physical body. If this is suspected, the projector should relax and let it happen, or use a projection technique like rope. A full projection can then occur if it has not already happened. Note: Many people are plagued by waking paralysis, and it can indeed be a terrifying experience, capable of causing psychological damage. Waking paralysis can best be broken by concentrating on a single big toe and trying hard to move it. Concentrate 'everything' on moving that big toe. Once this moves, even a tiny bit, full physical movement will be instantly restored.

Unwanted Vibrations & Projection Symptoms:

Frequent bouts of vibrations, waking paralysis and other projection related symptoms are a big problem for some people. Many people do not like these sensations and some can be absolutely terrified by them. Because of this, many people avoid sleep as a way of avoiding the projection symptoms, or other projection related problems, like bad oobe experiences or nightmares. This is the very worse thing they could do as this will have the reverse effect, and will greatly worsen the condition.

1. Lack of sleep causes over tiredness which encourages projection symptoms.
2. Sleeping flat on back encourages projection symptoms.
3. Hunger raises vibrations and encourages projection symptoms.

Lack of sleep can also cause a loss of appetite which can further aggravate this debilitating condition. Together with disturbing energy sensations and bad OOBE experiences, this can set up a psychological reflex and a physical condition which can progressively worsen the longer it is allowed to continue.

*The very first thing to address in cases like this is the
lack of sleep, which is the 'root' cause of the whole problem. I strongly suggest sufferers of this condition seek
medical advice 'urgently' and to ask for a strong enough
sleeping medication which will promote long lasting
and dreamless sleep. (I suggest people tell their doctor
they are suffering from insomnia caused by bad dreams
-which is partly true - to save lengthy explanations)
Once the sleep deficit is overcome and normal sleep
patterns return to normal, appetite will return and the
projection related symptoms will quickly cease.*

*Keep in mind here that the medication must be taken
regularly (as per medical advice) until the sleep deficit
is completely overcome before the medication can be
stopped, or the problem may reoccur.*

*If the use of medication is not possible, I suggest getting
up early in the morning and undertaking more physical
exercise than usual. This will 'naturally' tire out the
physical body, making for easier and heavier sleep.
This type of natural tiredness is quite different from 'over
tiredness' caused by a sleep deficit that has been built
up over a long time. The biggest problem with waking*

paralysis and OBE exit symptoms is that these 'wake
up' the physical body and mind. Therefore, if the physical body and mind are 'naturally' very tired, they will
not wake so easily, and waking paralysis and etc. will
be slept through, instead of them disturbing sleep and
causing fear episodes, etc.

Heavy Exit Sensations:

Heavy exit sensations, including the famous vibrations,
are simply energy movement sensations. The strength
of these, however, appears to be caused by the attempt
to shift the centre of 'waking' consciousness outside' the
bounds of the physical body, along with the real time
body as it projects. This forces a reflection of 'waking'
consciousness to go with the projecting double as it projects 'outside' the physical body. This throws a spanner
into the normal 'sleep projection' mechanism, and causes
a type of teeth rattling bio-energetic jarring to occur in
the physical/etheric body as it tries to accommodate the
unusual demand placed upon it. Normally, this shift of
reflected consciousness would follow the real time body,
outside the bounds of the physical body, naturally, while
falling asleep. This causes far lighter and less noticeable
energy movement sensations - i.e., not enough to

disturb the 'falling asleep' process. It is the presence of 'awake' consciousness during the projection process which causes all the problems.

it seems that maintaining two awake and active copies of consciousness, both interior and exterior, requires a great deal more energy flow than nature generally provides for, and this in itself appears to be the real cause of heavy exit sensations. This is, in other words, a true complication of consciousness, of spirit incarnation into a bio-energetic vehicle. I know this may sound like the same thing - a natural shift of 'falling asleep' consciousness out of body, as when compared with a deliberate shift of awake onsciousness out of body - but there is a vast difference in the energy requirements and resulting sensations for each. When a projector succeeds in shifting their centre of awareness strongly enough along 'with' their projecting double, there is also much more likelihood of them retaining their OOBE memories after re-entry and reintegration - when they wake up. Heavy exit sensations quickly reduce after the first few conscious exit projections, through forced bio-energetic development. The energy body progressively becomes used to the conscious exit process, and steadily adapts and develops in response to further awake OBE attempts, to provide for and handle the required energies.

Torso Energy Surge:

Many projections are ruined by a surge of energy in the torso, as energy flows through the legs and lower primary centres, through the navel and solar plexus to the heart and higher centres. This feels very much like the 'falling' sensation you get occasionally while drifting off to sleep. This feeling makes you catch at the sides of the bed, as if to stop yourself from falling.

All these sensations are caused by a surge of emotional type energy through the energy body and heart centre, as the real time double is generated and the projection out of body begins.

This sensation is so strong in some people it leaves them breathless and wide awake, thus breaking the delicate relaxed state necessary for conscious exit oobe. This can be an infuriating problem. The torso energy surge often contains a great deal of emotional, nervous and adrenalin affecting energies as massive amounts of energy move through the lower primary centres into and through the heart centre. This can be felt in much the same way as any emotional surging type of body-rush would be felt... like a huge wave of excitement, much like you may feel if you suddenly won a million dollars, or like the feelings caused by riding roller coaster or bungeejumping.

Sexual arousal is, also, not uncommonly related to this type of energy surge, as there is a primary energy centre (major chakra) situated directly over the genitals. (This centre is not mentioned in the Treatise, but is dealt with in my book "Astral Dynamics" under the Core Skills & Energy section) A strong upwards energy rush of energy will thus often involve this genital centre, to a greater or lesser extent, depending upon the energy make-up of the projector. Arousal usually breaks the delicately balanced state required for conscious exit oobe.

Lying prone on the back seems to intensify the torso energy surge problem. One way of easing this problem is to experiment with other resting/projection positions, to find one where the sensations are weaker or less distracting. These sensations are generally weaker when lying on your side or when sitting semi-upright. Lying fully on your side, however, tends to promote lucid dreams rather than OOBE's.

This energy surge is, basically, caused by massive energy movement through the energy body and its primary centres (major chakras). Heavy energy movement sensations are caused by energy blockages in energy structures not accustomed to conscious exit projection. The heavier the sensations the stronger will be the energy blockages causing them. When the energy body is unused to heavy primary centre energy movement, and the projector is awake, these sensations can severely disrupt projection attempts. The only way to solve this particular problem appears to be regular meditation, relaxation, trance & energy work, which promotes energy body development. This is best done separately from actual projection attempts.

These exercises should be continued until energy centres and their connecting pathways grow strong enough to handle the stronger energy movements which happen during a conscious exit oobe.

Lost Focus During The Exit:
A common cause of failed projection appears to be a failure to shift the 'centre' of consciousness out of the physical body along 'with' the real time double as it projects free of the physical body. It is extremely important a

projector keep their mind clear and focused on the action and sensation of leaving their physical body, to go with it, and not to lose touch with what is happening. Heavy exit sensations can make this difficult, I know, but they must be 'totally' ignored. Stay focused on the projection and where the centre of consciousness is going. If concentration slips at the wrong time, the real time body can project out, without a strong centre of waking consciousness. A reflection of mind will still transfer into the projecting real time double, but the projector's strongest centre of consciousness will, in effect, remain behind locked inside the physical/etheric body. This copy will be, in effect, left behind, feeling some degree of paralysis and weakness, thinking it has failed the projection completely, and will usually fall asleep shortly afterwards. In this case, strong memories are created in the physical brain, for the same time period as the projection. The projected double's memories can thus have trouble overwriting these upon reintegration. The whole idea, with this aspect of projection, is to make the 'projection' memories the strongest and most memorable memories for the same time period.

The above is a complication of the mind split effect

which causes enormous problems for projectors. It goes a long way to explaining what may have occurred when (as happens to many people) everything goes fine right up until the exit stage, with all the right sensations: vibrations, rapid heartbeat, falling or floating sensation, etc., and then everything just stops. It just goes away, leaving the almost-projector lying there wondering what happened and why they failed. Most people this happens to also feel exhausted, or partially or fully paralysed, after their seemingly failed projection attempt and soon fall into a deep sleep. The projection, in this case, will proceed without them, being centred in their projected double, without them being aware they have succeeded. In most cases, no memory of the successful projection will be evident upon waking.

FEAR has many colours:
1. Fear of heavy projection exit sensations.
2. Fear of the unknown out of body environment.
3. Religion instilled worry/fear of doing the wrong thing.

Fear has many subtle forms. All of these can be progressively overcome by understanding the mechanics and dynamics of OOBE and by experiencing the projected state at first hand. Projection out of body requires some bravery and fear is one of the first natural barriers faced by all new projectors standing on the threshold of a conscious exit projection. Fear is a natural barrier, apparently designed to stop people projecting until they are psychologically ready to operate out of their bodies. "True bravery is not the ability to fee! No fear, but is the ability to control fear whilst continuing to function in a reasonably normal fashion (RB). During an oobe, a projector is virtually invulnerable and can pass through solid matter, sit on ground zero during an atomic blast, or even to bask within the heart of a supernova unscathed. The only thing to fear while out of body is 'fear' itself. Nothing else can directly hurt a projector and nothing can get at their physical body and mind during a conscious projection. While it is fairly rare to come across anything nasty or negative during a projection, any troublesome entity a projector might stumble across cannot, therefore, directly harm them. They can, however, show themselves as a form designed to scare the daylights out of a projector, and this can cause psychologically damage. This can also result in a subconscious fear of OOBE.

*It can cause an instinctive, negative baulking type of
reaction which can ruining every conscious exit. This
can stop a projector from enjoying conscious OOBE for
the remainder of their life, unless they can program
themselves to overcome it. If this is already the case, I
suggest a course of affirmations and self hypnosis be
used to overcome it.*

Fear Of OOBE Exit Sensations:

*Fear of OOBE exit sensations is the very first of the
natural barriers to conscious exit oobe needed to overcome. This is not easy and can take a lot of control, as
well as a lot of faith that the heavy physical sensations
of early conscious projections will not actually hurt you.
The sensations can be extremely' physical and violent,
especially during the first few conscious exit attempts,
but will always progressively reduce during subsequent
projections.*

*The physical heartbeat is 'not' actually increased by
a conscious exit projection attempt. it is not 'caused'
to physically race by the OOBE attempt - although it
will often definitely 'feel' like it is racing so fast it seems
about to explode. This racing sensation is the heart*

chakra (primary centre) working overtime to provide the energy needed to generate and project the Real Time vehicle. The difficulty here is, again, caused by the real time body attempting to take an 'awake' copy of consciousness out of body. This is something quite different from natural sleep projection, and therefore can cause some rather extreme energy movement sensations, which are often felt as extremely physical sensations.

The heart may, indeed, increase in speed when the heart chakra becomes fully active 'if' the projector becomes frightened. Fear and panic can cause further sensations by way of an 'actual' rapid heartbeat, shortness of breath, vertigo, nausea, cramps and pain, etc. The best way to get over this is to concentrate everything on climbing ROPE and getting out of body as 'quickly' as possible - while totally ignoring the racing heart sensation and heavy bodily vibrations. The sooner the projector gets out of their body the sooner these will stop. The heavy physical sensations can, to a great extent, be reduced by regular meditation and energy work, which progressively develops the energy body, enabling it to provide and deal with the energies required for conscious exit projection. A smooth and rapid exit from the physical body is, *however, the very best way of overcoming this.*

Please note that 'not' everybody experiences heavy exit sensations, but it is far better to be prepared for a worst case scenario than to be caught by surprise and scared out of a perfectly good projection. Heavy exit sensations, on their own, can also cause psychological scarring and make each future projection attempt even more difficult to achieve. This is like how you might wince by instinctive reflex action while brushing a once sensitive tooth, even long after it has been repaired and no pain will be felt.

Fear Of The Unknown Out Of Body Environment:
Fear of the out of body environment itself is not easy to get over. This is simply caused by fear of the unknown and most people get some degree of this the first few times they get out. This type of fear seems related to the natural fear of the dark which all children have to grow out of This type of fear goes away gradually, as you become accustomed to projection sensations and the out of body environment through progressive personal experience. A new projector must be brave and control and ignore this fear, if only for a short time. Even if they still feel strong feelings of fear, they can and must ignore these and go on with their OOBE attempt. Once they get

out of body, they'll have overcome the first great barrier to OOBE and fear levels will be greatly reduced the next time they get out. Becoming progressively more and more familiar with the out of body environment, through multiple projections, is of the best ways of overcoming this type of fear.

Getting out, if only briefly and for the very first time, is the most important goal for any new projector. This will make the out of body environment much more real and it will make it even more achievable next time. Even if a projector only manages the conscious exit a couple of times, the memory and 'reality' of OOBE will be forever instilled into them by those experiences. The knowledge that they can exist apart from their physical body and remain intact, alive and functioning, will remain with them forever.

This, on its own, can also greatly help to reduce the fear of personal death, and even the pain of grief felt when a loved one is lost. OOBE provides very attainable firsthand experience of what it will be like to die. What is death if not the final projection out of body? If OOBE has been experienced, therefore, they are not going to *some strange place or having some totally unknown experience, i.e., death. They are only repeating (albeit with slightly more finality) something they have already experienced before.*

Projecting during daylight hours is the very best way to quickly overcome fear of the out of body environment. There is 'nothing' scary about flying around out of body on a bright sunny day. It's an enormously enjoyable experience, to say the very least. Have you ever wondered what it would be like to fly like Superman? And, if you worry about meeting something scary: I have never seen or heard of any type of negative or troublesome entity, not even the simple mischievous types, operating out in the open in full sunlight.

While it is possible to come across some things inside a building, the chances of meeting something scary are extremely remote if, after the exit, the projector immediately heads outside into the open and into the full sunlight.

The action of doing this quickly, immediately after the exit, may also throw a projector straight into the astral planes, again greatly reducing the likelihood of meeting anything scary.

Religion Instilled Worry/Fear:

Many people worry they are breaking God's laws, or infringing upon something in the Bible, by having OBE's. There are NO direct Biblical references which directly state projection is wrong, evil or even advising against it. In fact, there are many references within the bible that mention OBE, i.e., if memory serves me, St Paul speaks on this, when telling of one man's mystical experience: "whether in or out of his body I cannot tell".

If it's not written in the Holy Bible then it 'must' be evil is another common lame against OBE. However, the majority of the technological accomplishments of the modern world are also 'not' in the Bible. This does not make them evil in any way. OBE is witchcraft, as witches are known to have OBE's, and they therefore must be evil is another popular flame against OBE. Well, this is like saying that air travel is evil, simply because Hitler was known to fly in aircraft, or that the night is evil, simply because witches are generally more active at night, or that explosives are evil, simply because some people make bombs out of them to hurt people with.

My way of seeing this is: God created the heavens and the universe and everything within them. His creation is perfect and nothing has been overlooked, down to the smallest atom. God also created the integrated physical and energetic subtle bodies within man, and unseen inside His design lays the potential for the natural multi-dimensional mind split effect, which occurs to 'everyone' whenever they sleep. The ability to have conscious out of body experiences is a 'natural' ability and, even though many people find it difficult to accomplish, everyone has the potential for this ability. I think, if God did not want people to have OOBE's, He would have designed us a little differently, and made projection impossible? To think otherwise is to claim that God made a mistake, which is to say God is fallible, which is definitely irreligious and probably goes against all known religious and Biblical laws. My life experience leads me to sincerely believe that God is wise and that HE never ever makes mistakes.

Calling For Help:

It is possible to call for help from another projector when attempting to project, or to call someone to meet you when you get out of body. Once you hit the trance state, or feel heavy and are close to falling asleep, mentally call out the person's name several times, as loudly (mentally) as you can. If they are out of body they will definitely hear you, no matter where they are or how far away them might be, and will be drawn to come visit you. If this person is experienced, they may be able to help you out of your body. Another projector, although they may be able to help in other ways, will not, however, be able to actually 'pull' another projector out of their body. Any attempt to do so will be perceived by the projector as a psychic/energy body attack (very unpleasant cold shivers, etc.) which will tend to break their delicately balanced 'projectable' state. A projector can best help another projector by waiting for the natural projection (sleep projection) to take place and then making them aware they are projecting, helping them to remember it. Good advice at this time would be for them to dive back into their physical body shouting "I did it!" to help them cement their oobe memories.

Often, when a natural projection occurs, the real time body will drift slowly out of its physical body and hover just above it, mimicking its sleeping position. The real time projector in this state is asleep, just as its physical body and mind are. A helpful projector can best help them attain an OOBE by gently waking the sleeping projector's real time body and urging them to re-enter their physical body before it falls too deeply asleep. If this has already happened, a joint projection can then proceed. In this case, I suggest the novice projector periodically returns to their physical body and keeps a close eye on the time. They can then make sure they are hovering nearby and ready to dive back into their physical body shouting "I did it!" the moment the alarm clock starts to go off, when they feel the first tugs from the physical body as it begins reeling them in for reintegration.

Spirits:

Personally, I do not advise projectors call out to 'unknown' spirits or 'unknown' guides to help them project, unless they know 'exactly' who or what they are calling, and can verify their credentials as to exactly who and what they are. Calling blindly for any help from anywhere carries a high risk of attracting the unwanted attention of undesirable astral wildlife and mischievous spirit entities. Most types of intelligent astral wildlife and spirit entities appear to require some kind of 'permission' before they can interfere with a living person's life. Calling blindly for help can provide an entity with all the 'permission' it needs, albeit obtusely. And, once permission is given in cases like this, it cannot so simply or easily be revoked.

It is, I believe, a very unsafe practice indeed, to deliberately solicit the help of unknown spirit entities, as any type of open invite or request for help may invite a negative entity to trouble you instead.

Calling upon Angels, however, does not carry the same cautions as does blindly calling upon unknown spirits. Prayers to God (in whatever form or name you believe in) asking for His protection and help, however, are 'highly' recommended and do not carry this same risk. I thoroughly recommend a prayer for protection be 'sincerely' said before any projection, even just a few words, regardless of belief or religion - or even the lack of it. Prayers are most effective when said from a deeply re-

laxed 'quiet' mental state; i.e., from in the trance state. if a spirit of some kind does manifest during an OBE, and the projector is not sure if they are genuine or not, a simple test is to ask it to go away and leave you alone, and to return at another time, when called upon. Any good spirit will obey this request, and will return another time when called upon. If a spirit does not leave, or argues against this request, saying it knows better than you what's good for you, etc., then it's a pretty safe bet this spirit is not who they say they are.

There are certain skills necessary to be learned by any projector wishing to OOBE at will. There are 'no' safe short cuts to projection. The difficulties associated with conscious exit OOBE are best thought of as natural barriers, barriers which are there for a 'reason' and which are therefore unwise to avoid. If there is a friendly spirit or guide associated or interested in the progress of a projector, and they are interested in helping, they will know 'exactly' what the projector is doing and 'when' they are doing it. If they are willing and able to help with them learning projection, they will do so, without any request from the projector.

*The difficulties of conscious exit OOBE are 'natural'
barriers and it is unwise to avoid the lessons these hold
and the skills that can be gained in overcoming them.
These skills: deep physical relaxation, clearing the mind,
concentration, trance, bodily awareness actions, energy
raising and the ability to overcome fear, are necessary
requirements for successful and safe out of body operations. In a nutshell, if you cannot make it out of your
body under your own steam, you should not be projecting at that time. This does not, however, mean you
should not keep trying, as once the necessary skills
are learned, and you have fulfilled the requirements for
OBE operations, you will have passed the first natural
barrier and will be ready to take your first steps out of
your body.*

Physical Body's Eyes:

*While this may appear obvious to many people, I have
had a lot of queries over this matter. The physical body's
eyes must remain closed at all times during a projection
attempt. (You wouldn't believe how many times I've
been asked about this :) Real Time and/or Astral sight
will enable by itself during or just prior to a conscious
projection exit. If a projection is too dark or the pro-*

jector feels they are blind, I suggest they use the out of body energy raising techniques, as given earlier. It is also possible to create light by visualisation, by visualising a torch or lamp, etc. Many people find they simply have to ask for their sight when out of body and they get it straight away. Another way to overcome darkness is to visualise a well lit destination and use the instant travel method to project there.

REM (Rapid Eye Movement)

Rapid Eye Movement, commonly called the 'REM' state, often happens during an oobe attempt - often, but not always. This is a natural event triggered by the trance state when the physical body is very tired - when the physical body falls into a deeper sleep than is actually required, but with the mind still being held awake. The REM condition signposts the ideal time to have a lucid dream, as this indicates the dream mind is becoming active. If fear or other difficulties make OOBE difficult I suggest the projector focus on having a lucid dream at this time, as this will give some type of related out of body experience which will help prepare them for a full blown conscious exit OOBE later on. At this time a 'conscious' lucid dream becomes a viable alternative to a conscious OOBE, especially if REM activity is disturbing and breaking the concentration of the projector. Keep in mindhere that a lucid dream can be converted into a Real Time or astral projection if the projector focuses on and 'feels' for their body. They will then either project back to their body, or near to it, and a full OOBE can continue, or is then much easier to attain.

LD Note: A good way to attain a lucid dream, if lying down when the REM state hits, is for the projector to stop the OOBE attempt, staying relaxed and turning on their side (not their back) and to imagine a department store setting while allowing themselves to sink gently into sleep. If all goes well, they'll slip directly into a lucid dream with no apparent break in consciousness.

Closing Energy Centres?

Author's Note This section contradicts, corrects and replaces an earlier section in the original Treatise - on closing primary energy centres after using them. The reason for this contradiction is simply that my continuing research has led to an increased understanding of the energy body and how it works - with experience teaching me otherwise in this case:). After any type of

*energy work it is, traditionally, believed to be important
to close all energy centres that have been stimulated or
opened. While this idea appears to have some merit on
the surface, I have come to the conclusion it is a completely illogical practice. No localised awareness action
or visualised action can cause an energy centre (chakra)
to deactivate or close. This applies to any type of energy
centre, secondary or primary.*

*Experience tells me that no matter how an awareness
action is performed at the site of an energy centre it
will 'always' cause stimulation. It is a mistake to think
that any awareness or visualised action can succeed at
closing or deactivating an energy centre. This is a little
like fanning a spark (inactive energy centre) into a flame
with an stimulation action (making the spark an 'active'
energy centre) and then trying to make that same flame
go out by blowing up on it from a different direction.
However it is done, it will continue to fan the flame.
Consider this: Most popular chakra opening methods
involve visualising a small door or pair of curtains
opening over the site of a chakra. Once this is done that
chakra is deemed to have been 'opened'. This method
is then simply reversed to 'close' that chakra at the end*

of the session. Once these doors have been visualised as closing, the chakras are deemed to have been `closed'. Primary chakras are complex non-physical 'vortexes' of energy, each with a great many functions, about the size of the palm of your hand. If you look at just how a visualised 'little door' opening technique like this would affect a powerful energy structure like this, it becomes fairly obvious that a reversed action of 'closing' a simple little door would have little or no effect. It would also not affect it in the desired way. If you understand how bodily awareness and Tactile Imaging works, as per the Treatise, it becomes clear this reasoning is somewhat faulty. Both opening and closing methods involve a visu-alised or bodily awareness action at the site of a major chakra.

Both opening and closing actions will, therefore, each cause some degree of stimulation. Primary energy cen-tres cannot be likened to simple mechanical devices that can be switched off or closed by any such visualisation or awareness action.

Energy centres are, I think I have shown, not simply little doorways that can be opened and shut with good intentions and a little visualisation. Some people may dispute this, as energy centres are 'traditionally' supposed to be closed after use; as per popular new-age type theories and literature on this subject. Be that as it may, my logic is sound and based on repeatable experiments, and energy centres simply 'cannot' be deactivated or 'closed' in this way. If a person thinks they have succeeded at doing this, they will find this is merely a coincidence, and that the energy centres in question were deactivating on their own anyway. In most cases, primary energy centres will begin deactivating very quickly from the moment relaxation discipline is broken, when physical body movement and normal levels of mental activity are restored.

Reversing the energy 'raising' action and taking energy down through the legs (not through primary centres) however, does help reduce activity in primary energy centres. This reversed energy raising action does not involved any type of direct chakra stimulation and will reduces the amount of energy flowing into the energy body, especially through the legs. This reduces the amount of energy available to primary energy centres, thereby reducing activity in them to some extent. This does not, however, involve any focused awareness actions at the sites of primary centres.

Energy centres, primary and secondary, naturally reduce their level of activity once relaxation discipline is broken, as well as when they cease to be stimulated or used. The best way to deactivate energy centres is to stop stimulating and using them. Energy centres will also cease activity when they become energetically exhausted. This will happen when the supporting energy body circuitry shuts down, becomes exhausted, or for some other reason becomes incapable of providing the required energy flow necessary to maintain primary energy centres in their active state.

Note: if no significant continuing energy movement or activity is felt in primary energy centres, after a development session or projection attempt, they should be left alone. An attempt should be made to reduce activity 'only' if continuing chakra sensations are pronounced or become bothersome and uncomfortable. If left alone, they will naturally deactivate very quickly once relaxation discipline is broken and physical movement and activity are restored.

Ways Of Reducing Primary Centre Activity:

1. Reverse the energy raising action in the legs and arms alone - pushing energy back down and out of the body.

2. Stop focusing awareness on any primary energy centres.

3. Break mental relaxation and trance and restore normal physical and mental activity. Move, stand, talk, stretch and restore full circulation and movement.

4. Curl up and go to sleep - if this is appropriate.

5. Have a substantial snack or meal.

6. Press and hug a pillow into an uncomfortably over-active centre, then go to sleep or take a nap.

7. Vigorously rub, massage or slap the sites of overactive energy centres.

8. Physical exercise, like walking, jogging, swimming, aerobics, etc.

9. Take a shower - cold if necessary.

** Combinations of the above actions will slow or stop energy centre activity.*

YO-YO OOBE Technique:

The whole point of any OOBE technique is to exteriorize bodily awareness outside of the physical body to trigger the projection reflex quickly, whilst the projector remains mentally awake. This, apparently simple, awareness action can, however, be extremely difficult for most people to maintain for more than a couple of seconds. If this is done only briefly, however, over and over and rhythmically, for long enough, it will also have the effect of triggering the projection reflex.

Following is the outline of a new technique I call YOYO. I have used this myself and it seems to have almost as many good points as the Rope technique, but most people find YOYO much easier. This method is a good alternative if you are having trouble with ROPE. This can also be used as a good preparatory exercise for an OOBE attempt. It helps 'loosen up' the projectable double, even if another technique is to be used for the actual exit.

4. Get yourself into a deeply relaxed state, or into the trance state if possible, as you normally would prepare for using an OOBE technique.

1. Pick a target on the ceiling above your bed, or on the wall if using a chair.

This can be a light fitting or picture (anything) or you can tape a small paper target up above you.

2. Stand on a chair (careful not to fall) and get the feel of what it is like to have your face up close to the target. Feel the changed spatial coordinates.

Feel what this new position (up next to the target) feels like from there. Feel where the floor and bed and furniture and windows and doors are now.

Memorise what it 'feels' like to be in this position, up close to your target.

3. Instead of using ROPE, shift your awareness out of your body and push it right up next to the target, as if target were right next to your face.

Imagine and 'feel' yourself being at the target, right up close to it. Hold your awareness there for one second only and then pull your point of awareness back to your body. Feel yourself move right up to the target and, briefly, feel your spatial coordinates in the room change as your bodily awareness changes location. Feel the room move around you, briefly, as you fly up to the target and back to your body. Feel the room change back to normal when you pull your centre of awareness back to your body.

4. Bounce your awareness back and forth between the target and your body at roughly one second intervals (whatever feels most natural). Try and develop a natural rhythm, in and out, in and out, over and over.

5. When you get used to using this technique, extend your time at the target slightly, just a little bit longer. Always keep this time short enough to be comfortable and achievable so you can do it repeatedly, over and over, with ease. This takes concentration but is quite easy when you get the hang of it.

6. Keep this up and it will trigger the projection reflex just like ROPE.

7. Vary this technique as you see fit, with other OOBE techniques like ROPE, or rolling out of your body, or feeling yourself floating out of body, point shift, etc. You may, for example, trigger the projectable state, feeling vibrations, etc., using YOYO and find it easier to finish off the exit using ROPE, or by rolling out of your body, or with another favourite method.

Racing Heartbeat, Disorientation & Pressure:
In my opinion, disorientation and head pressure, during or after an OBE or OBE attempt, stem from forced bio-energetic development, caused by an OBE attempt. Any problems resulting from this will settle down over a couple of days. I do not advise further attempts until you feel completely normal again - as things must have time to adjust and develop in response to what has happened -as a muscle must be given time to heal and develop after being overworked and strained.

While a logical observation, and partly true, the assumption that the heart chakra is not getting enough energy, and that this is causing it to race during an OBE attempt, is not entirely correct. This matter is far more complex than it appears.

When you cease a projection causing bodily awareness action, i.e., Rope, and observe the throbbing in your heart chakra slowing, you have actually eased the pressure that was forcing your energy body to generate your projectable double. This eases the load on the heart chakra, thus slowing its activity.

The heart chakra is forced to provide a lot of energy, to generate the projectable double, during an awake induced OBE attempt. Excessive heart centre activity, and all other heavy exit sensations, are 'caused' by the presence of 'awake' consciousness, which cause a plethora of bio-energetic conflicts to arise. To support this: think how easily you project out of body when your mind is asleep, and out of the bio-energetic equation? When asleep, you'll find you slip out with hardly a murmur from your hear chakra, feeling only a mild, brief falling sensation. At the very worse this level of exit sensations will make you catch the sides of your bed, especially at times when you are drifting in and out of sleep, before actually falling asleep.

When awake consciousness is present during an OBE attempt, a true 'complication of bio-incarnated cons-

ciousness' arises. Your awake mind changes the whole equation, and the usual bio-energetic projection mechanism comes under a lot of unusual pressure. It finds it must work overtime to provide the energies needed to generate the projected double while awake consciousness is present. When awake consciousness is present during projection, the bio-energetic projection mechanism has to overcome the awake mind's conscious control over its physical body, and the 'tension' this automatically generates.

By partly true, I mean that the heart chakra does speed up when increased energy demands are placed upon it. This can occur during an OBE, when the projected double deliberately draws more energy from its physical/ etheric counterpart, which is energetically maintaining its projected double via the Silver Cord. A noticeable heavier thrumming will also be felt from within the perceived chest area of the projected double when this happens, even though it does not have a chest, per se. This is especially noticeable at close range, within 20 feet (6 metres) or so, during a Real Time OBE, and eases with greater distance.

But, when heart centre throbbing speeds up during a conscious exit OBE attempt (which is especially noticeable during early OBE's and OBE attempts), this is a sign that awake consciousness is throwing a spanner into the works, so to speak.

Apart from the 'unavoidable' presence of awake consciousness - which must be overcome through repeated OBE attempt experience (which develops the projection mechanism to the point where it can compensate), plus simple bio-energetic development - most of the problems this causes stem from a lack of deep physical relaxation. This is the most 'widespread' problem and general cause of this. The vast majority of would-be projectors do not attain a sufficient state of deep physical relaxation prior to OBE attempts, and then experience heavy exit sensations and problems as a result. No way! You might say, "I'm in full trance and so 'must' be deeply physically relaxed enough for projection to occur. Well, while an understandable assumption, think on this: it is quite possible to attain a fairly deep level of trance (usual y too deep for easy OBE) while the physical body still retains sufficient physical tension to interfere with the projection mechanism. In a similar way, it is also possible to fall asleep while still full of stress and tension. For example, I can attain a full trance state while standing and even walking - which obviously entails physical tension, which obviously would interfere with an OBE attempt, if I attempted one at this time.

My suggestion is to read The Treatise on OBE, Version 2.00, parts 1 - 8, and then to spend at least a few weeks practising deep physical relaxation, and trance work only. Do this 'separately' from OBE attempts, preferably at times when you are wide awake, like in the morning. This makes relaxation and trance work much harder, but has far more development benefits because of this. If after following the above advice, you still have problems, I'd consider the Mind-Split as being the culprit stopping you from 'remembering' your OBE's. If you experience vibrations or other exit sensations prior to the racing heart centre sensation, it possible that you had already succeeded at projecting, but had missed the exit: meaning that after your projected double had departed, your physical/etheric aspect was continuing to attempt projection. Under this circumstance, projection is impossible, re the etheric body cannot leave its physical counterpart while an OBE is 'already' in progress.

Emotion & Re-entry:

The emotional content of the re-entry phase is 'extremely' important as it strengthens OBE memories. If the mind split is responsible, and it probably is, for failed OBE attempts, this means your memories of existing in your physical/etheric body are not allowing your OBE memories to 'overwrite' them after re-entry. The nature of the physical brain is to record only a single memory for any single time period. During an OBE, two completely separate sets of memory are present - those of the physical/etheric body and those of its projected double. The 'strongest' memory set will be the set retained, as a recallable memory, after an OBE. The memories of the physical/etheric body have more of an immediate impact on the physical brain, as these memories are automatically recorded, as per normal physical memory recording. in order for an OBE memory download to take place, and overwrite these memories, they have to be stronger and have more 'impact' than the resident memories. Emotion can thus be used to empower OBE memories, to give them more impact on the physical brain. It is for the above reasons that fearful or exciting, more dramatic; OBE's are more easily remembered than are the more mundane type.

I remember during my early days of OBE (when I started doing it deliberately) floating near my physical body trying to work out why I seemed to be failing and losing the OBE memory most of the time. I was trying to OBE just about every night, but had only succeeded a few times that year. At these times, my projected double had no problem exiting my physical body. I wondered, as it was so easy, why I was not remembering more of my OBE's. Then I remembered how excited I was during and after these OBE's, and started to wonder....'hmmm, maybe emotion itself had something to do with carrying the OBE memories back into my physical body with me?'

I made a successful 'emotional' re-entry that night, and remembered my OBE reasoning. I have applied this reasoning ever since then, and have thus had countless successful OBE's. Now, I always 'shout' my success 'savagely' in some way as I make the re-entry. I hold the OBE memory very strongly in mind and use a trigger phrase to enforce an effective memory download, i.e., "I did it!" or "My hands melted!" or etc. This works! I always come to (wake up) with my trigger phrase on my lips, and with full memory of my OBE. This really does make a world of difference.

www.ingramcontent.com/pod-product-compliance
Lightning Source LLC
La Vergne TN
LVHW020323200726
843507LV00012B/2211